Myth Unleashed: Rediscovering the Legends of Hercules and the Pantheon

Myrddin Sage

Published by Myrddin Sage, 2024.

While every precaution has been taken in the preparation of this book, the publisher assumes no responsibility for errors or omissions, or for damages resulting from the use of the information contained herein.

MYTH UNLEASHED: REDISCOVERING THE LEGENDS OF HERCULES AND THE PANTHEON

First edition. July 8, 2024.

ISBN: 979-8227926050

Written by Myrddin Sage.

Table of Contents

Myth Unleashed: Rediscovering the Legends of Hercules and the Pantheon

Journey Through Time in Vivid Tales and Transform Your Understanding of Mythology Today

Preface

"Myths are public dreams, dreams are private myths." – Joseph Campbell.

As you turn the pages of this journey into the heart of ancient mythology, you'll find yourself walking alongside legends like Hercules and delving deep into the vibrant lives of the Gods and Demi-Gods that populate the Pantheon. This book is a tapestry woven with the threads of ancient tales, reimagined and retold to resonate with contemporary hearts and minds. My goal in writing this work was not just to recount these age-old stories but to transform them into a mirror reflecting our lives today, revealing timeless truths and insights that are as relevant as they were thousands of years ago.

I've always been mesmerized by how mythology serves as a bridge between the worlds of the past and the present. However, I realized that for many, these stories remain just beyond reach—locked within dense academic texts and obscured by archaic language. This realization struck a chord with me during a lecture series I attended. I witnessed a young student struggle to connect with the sheer vibrancy of Hercules' labors because of their dry presentation. It was then that the seeds for this book were sown. I envisioned a book that breaks down these barriers and dresses these tales not in scholarly robes but in vivid narrative and accessible prose.

Throughout my journey of bringing this book to life, I have been blessed with unyielding support and inspiration from various quarters. Esteemed historians and fellow mythology enthusiasts provided invaluable insights that helped shape this narrative. Their generous contributions have been nothing short of Herculean, and I am profoundly grateful.

By delving into this book, you embark on a voyage through time. Whether you are a humanities student, a history buff, or simply someone enchanted by the rich tapestry of mythological lore, there is something in these pages for you. Through engaging storytelling and thoughtful reflection on ancient narratives, I hope to offer you entertainment and enlightenment—a dual discovery of myth and self.

The journey we will take together does not require prior knowledge, just an open heart, and a curious mind. This exploration will connect dots from ancient myths to modern-day dilemmas, extracting lessons that transcend time.

I sincerely thank you for inviting me into your reading world. Your time and attention to these pages are gifts I receive with deep gratitude. As you continue reading, may you find yourself inspired, your thoughts provoked, and your heart stirred by the legendary exploits of gods and heroes.

Embark on this adventure with an open heart; let us rediscover together the echoes of old myths in our modern lives.

Chapter 1: Unveiling the New Myths

In the soft haze of the afternoon, Elena found herself in the middle of her grandmother's old study, a room heavy with the scent of aged paper and whispers of the past. The walls were lined with shelves that reached up towards the high ceiling, each shelf groaning under the weight of books bound in leather and cloth. Sunlight filtered through a dusty window, casting slanted beams across the faded Persian rug.

Elena ran her fingers over the spines of countless volumes, each embossed with titles that spoke of myths and legends from around the world. She paused at a mainly worn book; its cover cracked and pages yellowed with time. It was a collection of Greek myths, tales she had heard from her grandmother as a child — stories of gods and heroes, their triumphs and tragedies resonating through time.

As she opened to a random page, her eyes fell upon the story of Persephone. The tale spun in her mind, not just as it was written but as it might be told today: Persephone is a young woman caught between two worlds, and her story is one of empowerment rather than abduction. Elena imagined retelling this myth in modern prose, transforming ancient archetypes into characters that breathed and struggled in ways that mirrored contemporary life.

A creak outside the door interrupted her thoughts. Her younger brother Luca entered, his presence pulling her back to reality. "Are you still digging through grandma's old myths?" he asked with a smirk.

Elena nodded slowly. "There's something timeless about them," she replied. "But also something that begs for renewal."

Luca walked over to glance at the open page. "Like updating them for today's world? Making them relevant again?"

"Exactly," Elena said as she closed the book softly. "Imagine weaving these old stories into narratives that speak directly to us today — not just preserving them but revitalizing them."

They looked around at the myriad books surrounding them, each brimming with potential stories waiting to be reborn for modern readers.

As they stepped out into the waning light of day, leaving behind the sanctuary of aged lore, Elena pondered how such age-old wisdom could be transformed to guide us now. Could these revived tales help us navigate our complexities by reflecting on our past?

Why Myths Still Matter: Breathing New Life into Ancient Legends

In an era dominated by rapid technological advancements and global connectivity, the ancient myths of Hercules and the Pantheon might seem like relics of a bygone age. Yet, these stories, rich with heroism and human folly, hold timeless lessons that are still relevant today. The challenge, however, lies in making these tales resonate with contemporary audiences who might find the traditional narratives distant and unrelatable. This is where the art of reimagining these stories becomes vital. By infusing modern narrative techniques and contemporary language into these myths, we preserve their legacy and enhance their accessibility and appeal.

The task ahead is twofold: to unveil why it is crucial to reshape these ancient narratives for today's readership and to explore how this transformation can be achieved effectively. Through a detailed exploration of modern storytelling methods, this chapter demonstrates how classic myths can be transformed into engaging stories that captivate modern minds while retaining their profound philosophical depth.

Reimagining for Relevance

The primary reason behind reimagining mythological tales lies in their continued relevance. These stories offer more than just entertainment; they provide moral insights and reflect on human nature in ways applicable across ages. However, with adaptation, there is a risk that the wisdom embedded within them might be recovered to antiquity. Therefore, **revitalizing these narratives** ensures they remain a vibrant part of our cultural tapestry, offering insights and lessons pertinent to contemporary issues.

Modern Narratives for Timeless Lessons

Transforming these age-old tales involves more than updating the language; it requires reconceptualizing how they are told. This includes adopting new formats such as graphic novels, interactive media, or virtual reality experiences that can make Hercules' labors or Zeus' machinations more vivid and relatable. Such adaptations draw in new audiences and enrich the storytelling experience, allowing for deeper emotional engagement and a more personal connection with the myths.

Cultural Preservation Through Innovation

Moreover, this revitalization effort serves a larger purpose: preserving a cultural heritage. Myths carry cultural values and historical insights, acting as windows into the civilizations that created them. Keeping these myths alive and relevant ensures that future generations can also benefit from their wisdom and beauty. This chapter will explore how innovative narrative techniques can aid in this preservation while keeping the stories fresh and exciting.

Readers will understand the necessity and methods of transforming mythological narratives through this exploration. They will see how Hercules' strength can be a metaphor for personal resilience in modern times or how Athena's wisdom can provide guidance in an information-saturated age.

By approaching these ancient tales with reverence and creativity, we open up a world where mythology no longer feels like a subject confined to dusty library shelves but pulses vividly in our everyday lives. Through this book, you will journey back in time and deep into the human psyche, exploring themes of heroism, morality, and survival through the lens of Hercules and his fellow deities.

Thus begins our quest to unlock the power of myths in modern times, rekindling old flames with new sparks to illuminate past insights and present realities.

Traditional mythological tales have a timeless quality that resonates across generations. However, their presentation in academic texts often creates a barrier for modern audiences, making them seem outdated and inaccessible. **Reimagining these stories into engaging, contemporary narratives is essential to breathe new life into these ancient myths**. By transforming classic tales into captivating stories with modern language and formats, we can bridge the gap between the past and present, ensuring that these narratives remain relevant and impactful today.

Reimagining mythological tales makes them more relatable and enjoyable for contemporary audiences. We can unlock these stories' timeless wisdom and universal themes by infusing them with fresh perspectives and language. This process revitalizes the myths and allows readers to connect with the characters and lessons on a deeper level.

Through this transformation, ancient myths become vibrant, engaging narratives that resonate with modern sensibilities.

Revisiting traditional myths in a new light can offer profound insights and perspectives. By updating the language and presentation of these stories, we can uncover hidden meanings and relevance that may have been lost over time. **Reimagining mythological tales is a powerful way to keep cultural heritage alive** while providing valuable lessons and reflections for contemporary society.

In today's fast-paced world, where traditional forms of storytelling may struggle to capture attention, reimagining mythological tales offers a fresh approach to engage readers. **By presenting these timeless stories in a contemporary light**, we invite audiences to explore the depths of mythology in a way that feels relevant and exciting. **This shift in storytelling preserves ancient wisdom and encourages new generations to discover the magic of mythology in a way that speaks to them.**

Continue reading to explore how classic myths can be transformed into captivating contemporary narratives.

In mythology, breathing new life into ancient tales is a creative endeavor and a crucial step in preserving these stories for modern audiences. **Transforming classic myths into captivating contemporary narratives** involves a delicate balance between honoring the tales' original essence and making them accessible and engaging for today's readers.

One method for revitalizing mythological stories is to infuse them with relatable themes and emotions that resonate with contemporary experiences. By highlighting universal human struggles, such as love, betrayal, or ambition, these myths can transcend time and culture, speaking directly to readers' hearts. **Embedding modern dilemmas** within the narrative structure allows for a seamless connection between the ancient myth and the present-day world.

Another practical approach is to adapt the language and style of storytelling to suit current tastes and preferences. **Crafting vivid imagery** through descriptive language can transport readers into the mythical realms, immersing them in a sensory experience that feels familiar and enchanting. By using accessible language and relatable dialogue, these narratives become more inviting and relatable to a broader audience.

Moreover, **exploring diverse perspectives** within classic myths can offer fresh insights and angles that resonate with contemporary values. These narratives gain depth and complexity by delving into the motivations and emotions of lesser-known characters or reinterpreting well-known figures through a modern lens, inviting readers to contemplate nuanced moral dilemmas and ethical questions.

Additionally, **incorporating interactive elements into** mythological storytelling can enhance engagement and immersion for modern audiences. Whether through multimedia platforms, interactive websites, or immersive experiences, these adaptations bring myths to life in dynamic ways that cater to diverse learning styles and preferences.

By embracing creativity and innovation in the retelling of mythological tales, authors can bridge the gap between past traditions and present sensibilities, ensuring that these timeless stories remain vibrant and relevant today. Through thoughtful adaptation and imaginative reinterpretation, classic myths can continue to captivate audiences and offer profound insights into the human experience across cultures and generations.

In assessing how the revitalization of mythology can preserve cultural heritage and offer relevant teachings today, we uncover a treasure trove of wisdom waiting to be unearthed. **Mythology**, with its rich tapestry of stories and characters, mirrors ancient civilizations' values, beliefs, and struggles. By breathing new life into these age-old tales, we keep our cultural heritage alive and provide a roadmap for navigating the complexities of modern life.

Through the lens of mythology, we can gain profound insights into human nature, relationships, and the eternal battle between good and evil. These timeless themes resonate across centuries, bridging the gap between past and present. By revisiting these myths in a contemporary context, we invite a new generation to engage with narratives that have shaped societies for millennia.

The revitalization of mythology is not merely an exercise in storytelling; it is a means of preserving our collective memory and honoring the traditions of our ancestors. Just as oral traditions passed down these myths from generation to generation, our modern retellings ensure these tales continue to captivate and inspire audiences worldwide.

By infusing mythology with fresh perspectives, we can extract valuable lessons that are still relevant today. The trials and triumphs of mythological heroes parallel our struggles, reminding us of the enduring human spirit that transcends time and culture. Through these stories, we find solace, inspiration, and guidance in navigating the complexities of our modern world.

Moreover, the revitalization of mythology fosters a sense of connection to our roots, instilling pride in our cultural heritage and a deeper appreciation for the diverse tapestry of human experience. In a rapidly changing world where traditions often fade into obscurity, mythology is an anchor to our past, grounding us in shared narratives that bind us together as a global community.

As we embark on this journey to rediscover the myths that have shaped civilizations for centuries, we are reminded of the enduring power of storytelling to transcend time and space. By revitalizing mythology, we preserve our cultural legacy and pave the way for future generations to glean wisdom from the tales of old.

In conclusion, we ensure their teachings remain vibrant and relevant today by breathing new life into ancient myths. As we delve deeper into these captivating narratives, we unearth hidden treasures of knowledge and insight that enrich our lives and deepen our understanding of humanity's collective journey through time.

As we close this opening chapter, it's crucial to reflect on the vibrant journey we've embarked upon. By reimagining mythological tales for modern audiences, we breathe new life into these ancient narratives and ensure their survival and continued relevance in today's world. **Transforming classic myths into contemporary stories** allows us to preserve the rich tapestry of our cultural heritage while making it accessible and engaging for everyone.

The process of revitalizing mythology involves more than updating the language or setting; it's about weaving in themes and issues that resonate with current generations. This approach does not simply retell old stories but reinterprets and recontextualizes them, making timeless lessons applicable to modern-day challenges. Through this, myths can continue to offer profound insights about human nature and the world around us.

Looking ahead, the subsequent chapters of this book promise even deeper explorations into the legends of Hercules and the Pantheon. You will discover how these ancient characters and their adventures can provide valuable perspectives on bravery, resilience, and morality in contemporary settings. Each narrative revisited through a modern lens, offers not just entertainment but also a mirror reflecting our own lives and choices.

Let this journey be enlightening and inspiring, encouraging you to see these old stories through new eyes. As we delve deeper into the myths of yesteryears, let us carry forward the wisdom they encapsulate, helping us navigate the complexities of modern life with greater clarity and purpose. When reimagined thoughtfully, the stories of gods and heroes become not just tales of the past but guiding lights for our future.

Embrace this adventure with an open heart and mind, ready to rediscover and transform your understanding of mythology. Together, let's ensure that these legendary tales continue to inspire, teach, and resonate with us all, bridging the gap between the ancient and the contemporary in the most captivating ways possible.

Chapter 2: Hercules: A Mirror to Our Lives

In the cool shadow of the university library, Thomas sat alone at a worn wooden table. His eyes, usually bright with the spark of curiosity, today reflected a more profound, troubled contemplation. Around him, the hushed whispers of pages turning and distant footsteps on marble floors created a symphony of academia. But his mind was far from the texts on ancient mythology laid open before him; it wrestled instead with the weight of his own modern-day Herculean tasks.

Thomas had always found solace in antiquity's stories, drawing parallels between mythical heroes' quests and his personal challenges. As he ran his fingers over the lines describing Hercules' twelve labors, he couldn't help but see them as metaphors for his recent struggles at work, where he faced seemingly insurmountable tasks daily.

He thought about Hercules facing the Nemean Lion, using nothing but his strength and wit to overcome an invincible beast. Thomas likened this to tackling a project with impossible deadlines and uncooperative team members. Wasn't he, too, in some way, trying to find strength within himself to conquer beasts of modern bureaucracy?

A soft gust from an opening door carried in autumn's crisp breath and rustled through pages marked by ancient fingers. It reminded him that every season brings change, yet he was stuck in an endless cycle of stress and expectation.

As he glanced around the library, Thomas noted other students engrossed in their studies—each absorbed in their own world of academic or personal battles. He pondered how Hercules' quest for redemption through labor mirrored these students' quests for knowledge and achievement.

Suddenly, a laugh broke through his reverie—a group studying nearby shared a joke or perhaps solved a complex problem together.

It struck Thomas that Hercules, too, found moments of relief and companionship during his trials; possibly, there was room for lightness even within his own challenges.

The air grew denser as evening approached, casting long shadows across stone floors and ancient texts. Thomas closed his books slowly, feeling slightly more aligned with himself. Like Hercules, who found wisdom through suffering and perseverance, could we not grow through our trials?

As he packed up to leave under the watchful eyes of marble busts of philosophers long gone, one question lingered: In our pursuit to overcome personal labors like Hercules did long ago—are we not all searching for our own version of immortality?

Are the Trials of Hercules Still Testing Us Today?

The legend of Hercules, with his daunting labors and tumultuous life journey, transcends mere ancient storytelling to reflect more profound truths about the human condition. His trials are not just relics of a mythological past but are vibrant narratives that continue to resonate in the fabric of contemporary life. In this exploration, we aim to uncover how these age-old tales hold up a mirror to our modern existence, shedding light on universal themes and guiding us through personal and societal challenges.

Though steeped in the supernatural, Hercules' tasks symbolize everyday human experiences such as adversity, resilience, and the pursuit of identity and purpose. Each labor he undertook is a metaphor for our daily struggles—be it at home, in our careers, or within our inner psychological battles. By dissecting these myths, we can gain insights into how to navigate our lives with courage and determination.

Reflecting Modern Human Experiences Through Ancient Myths

The universality of Hercules' story is undeniable. Who among us has not faced a seemingly impossible challenge or been burdened by tasks that feel both endless and essential? These stories provide more than entertainment; they offer a blueprint of heroism that can be adapted to overcome our life's hurdles. This chapter delves into these parallels, drawing connections between Hercules' heroic journeys and the everyday heroics required in modern life.

Lessons from the Past Informing Present Dilemmas

Moreover, Hercules' experiences with betrayal and moral questioning are profoundly relevant today. In an era where ethical boundaries are continually tested in personal and professional realms, these myths offer valuable lessons on integrity and the consequences of our choices. Through Hercules' narrative, we can explore how ancient wisdom can inform contemporary decision-making and ethical judgments.

The Timeless Relevance of Myth in Understanding Human Behavior

It's fascinating to consider how ancient storytellers used myths like those of Hercules to process complex human emotions and societal issues. Today, these stories still serve as tools for understanding human behavior—highlighting patterns that have persisted across centuries. This chapter aims to unpack these patterns and apply them to understanding behaviors in modern contexts, such as leadership, resilience, and personal growth.

By revisiting these timeless tales, we reconnect with a shared cultural heritage and equip ourselves with enduring strategies for dealing with hardship and achieving personal excellence. The myth of Hercules encourages us to strive and reflect on what it truly means to be victorious in life's battles.

In weaving together the old with the new, this discussion will illuminate how mythology's essence is not trapped in the past but is alive—and deeply relevant—in the present. Through this reflective journey, we hope to inspire readers to embrace their challenges with renewed perspective and vigor.

In summary, as we traverse Hercules' legendary exploits, we uncover layers of human truth that continue to instruct and inspire. This chapter highlights these layers, connecting mythic themes with real-world applications and enriching our understanding of ancient tales and modern realities.

In the timeless stories of Hercules, we find reflections of our own struggles and triumphs, encapsulating universal themes that resonate deeply with modern human experiences. **Courage, betrayal, and the quest for meaning** are not merely ancient concepts but enduring facets of the human condition that continue to shape our lives today. The trials faced by Hercules mirror our own challenges, offering insights into how we navigate the complexities of existence.

Hercules' journey is marked by his extraordinary strength and courage. Yet, his humanity and vulnerabilities make him a relatable figure. His battles against formidable foes like the Hydra or the Nemean Lion symbolize the inner conflicts we face daily—the obstacles that seem impossible, the fears that threaten to overwhelm us. Through Hercules' struggles, we see a reflection of our internal battles, reminding us that **courage is not the absence of fear but the ability to face it head-on.**

The theme of betrayal runs deep in Hercules' stories, most notably in Hera's hostility towards him. Betrayal is a universal experience that cuts to the core of trust and loyalty. Like Hercules, we may be deceived or let down by those closest to us, grappling with hurt and disillusionment. However, it is in overcoming these betrayals that we discover our inner strength and resilience, forging a path toward **self-discovery** and **personal growth.**

At the heart of Hercules' myth lies the quest for meaning—a search for purpose and identity amidst life's uncertainties. This quest remains as relevant as ever in a world of distractions and noise. We constantly seek fulfillment and direction, striving to make sense of our place in the grand scheme. Hercules' journey is a poignant reminder that **true meaning is found not in external achievements but in inner transformation.**

Join us as we delve deeper into Hercules' stories to uncover timeless lessons and truths that resonate with our lives.

The tales of Hercules reflect our own personal and professional challenges. The struggles faced by the mythical hero resonate with the dilemmas we encounter in our daily lives. *Hercules' journey* teaches us about the importance of perseverance in the face of adversity. Just as Hercules had to overcome twelve arduous tasks, we, too, must tackle our own obstacles with determination and resilience.

Betrayal is a theme central to Hercules' story, mirroring the betrayals we may experience in our personal and professional relationships. Whether it is a friend's disloyalty or a colleague's deceit, these instances challenge our trust and integrity. Learning from Hercules, we understand that forgiveness is not a sign of weakness but a display of strength. We can reclaim our power and dignity by letting go of grudges and moving forward.

The quest for meaning, another prevalent motif in Hercules' myths, reflects our search for purpose and fulfillment. Just as Hercules sought to prove his worth through heroic deeds, we, too, strive to find significance in our lives. These stories remind us that true fulfillment comes from within, from aligning our actions with our values and beliefs.

Courage, perhaps Hercules's most celebrated quality, serves as a beacon for us in times of uncertainty and fear. The hero's fearless encounters with monsters and challenges inspire us to confront our fears head-on. By channeling our inner courage, we can navigate life's uncertainties with grace and determination.

Hercules' myths offer valuable lessons on leadership and integrity in both personal and professional spheres. The hero's unwavering commitment to his values exemplifies the importance of staying true to oneself even in the face of temptation or hardship. By embodying Hercules' virtues of honor and righteousness, we can inspire others and lead by example.

The consequences of Hercules' actions also remind us of the impact of our choices on ourselves and those around us. Our decisions shape our destiny, just as Hercules' deeds determined his fate. Reflecting on these stories prompts us to consider the moral implications of our actions and strive for virtuous conduct in all aspects of life.

As we delve deeper into *Hercules' narratives*, we uncover profound insights into human nature and behavior. The hero's struggles mirror our inner conflicts and ethical dilemmas, prompting us to reflect on our choices and motivations. By internalizing the timeless lessons embedded in these myths, we can navigate the complexities of modern life with wisdom and clarity.

Embracing the wisdom encapsulated in *Hercules' myths* allows us to transcend time and connect with universal truths that resonate across cultures and generations. These stories serve as mirrors reflecting our shared experiences, guiding us towards self-discovery and growth. Through introspection and reflection on Hercules' journey, we embark on a path of self-realization and transformation, drawing inspiration from ancient tales to navigate the challenges of today's world with courage and integrity.

Descriptive Framework: Hercules' Mythological Wisdom for Modern Life

This framework will explore how the timeless themes in Hercules' myths can be applied to contemporary human behavior and struggles. By dissecting key elements like strength, perseverance, humility, and redemption from Hercules' stories, readers can draw parallels to their own lives. Let's delve into each framework component to understand its significance and practical application.

Key Themes from Hercules' Myths

Strength: Both physical and moral strength are essential attributes in Hercules' tales. This theme emphasizes the importance of resilience and courage in facing life's challenges.

Perseverance: The myth of Hercules is rife with instances where he had to persist against all odds. This theme highlights the value of determination and persistence in overcoming obstacles.

Humility: Despite his extraordinary abilities, Hercules also faced moments of vulnerability and humility. This theme underscores the importance of staying grounded and recognizing one's limitations.

Redemption: Hercules' journey is marked by moments of redemption where he seeks to atone for past mistakes. This theme showcases the power of forgiveness, growth, and second chances.

Interpreting Hercules' Stories for Personal Reflection

Each theme from Hercules' myths can be dissected through specific stories or tasks from his adventures. Readers can reflect on these narratives by asking themselves interpretive questions that draw connections to their personal or professional experiences.

For instance, when examining Hercules' labor of slaying the Lernaean Hydra, one could reflect on recurring challenges in their career or personal growth. Questions like *"What recurring obstacles have I faced? How have I approached them? What innovative solutions have I employed?"* can help individuals draw parallels to their perseverance and problem-solving skills.

Practical Application and Reflective Writing

The framework encourages readers to engage in reflective writing by documenting instances where they have encountered similar themes. By doing so, individuals can gain deeper insights into how they've navigated challenges, displayed strength, perseverance, humility, or sought redemption.

Through reflective writing exercises, readers can actively apply mythological wisdom to their everyday lives, enhance their understanding of these ancient tales, and cultivate a deeper awareness of how universal themes manifest in their journeys.

Dynamics and Practical Implications

This framework is a practical tool for translating the age-old wisdom embedded in Hercules' myths into actionable insights for modern life. By exploring these themes and reflecting on personal experiences, individuals can harness the transformative power of mythological narratives to navigate their own struggles with courage, resilience, humility, and growth.

Through consistent engagement with this framework, readers can cultivate a more profound self-awareness and draw inspiration from Hercules' legendary exploits to face contemporary challenges with renewed vigor and wisdom.

Hercules' tales, with their intricate weave of challenges and triumphs, offer more than just entertainment; they serve as a profound guide for our personal and professional lives. These stories mirror our modern experiences, reflecting universal themes like courage in adversity and the pursuit for purpose. By delving into these myths, we gain a deeper understanding of ancient narratives and valuable insights into contemporary human behavior and struggles.

Hercules' journey underscores the importance of resilience and moral fortitude. Each labor he undertakes is not just a physical challenge but a moral one, prompting us to consider how we tackle our obstacles. Whether navigating office politics or personal relationships, the essence of his trials resonates with the tests we face today. The courage to confront these tasks, often against formidable odds, is as relevant now as it was in ancient times.

The relevance of these myths extends beyond historical interest; they are vital tools for introspection and growth. Reflecting on Hercules' choices and outcomes encourages us to examine our decisions and their alignment with our values. This introspective journey can lead to profound personal growth and improved interpersonal relationships, highlighting the timeless nature of these ancient lessons.

Moreover, Hercules' story is a testament to the human spirit's unyielding strength and capacity to overcome. It inspires us to pursue our goals relentlessly despite the hurdles we might encounter.

This motivational aspect of mythology can empower us to take bold steps in our lives, be it changing careers, starting new ventures, or simply standing up for what is right.

In sharing these tales, we connect with others through shared human experiences, fostering empathy and understanding across diverse life paths. These stories remind us that, though times may change, human existence's core challenges and triumphs remain constant.

By embracing these age-old narratives, we enrich our lives with wisdom that transcends generations. Let us continue to explore these myths, drawing lessons that inspire and guide us through the complexities of modern life. Through Hercules' stories, we find a reflection of our past and a beacon for our future.

Chapter 3: Beyond the Myth: Personal and Social Evolution

In the heart of a bustling city filled with the constant hum of life, Thomas walked briskly through the crowded streets. His mind was as cluttered as the sidewalks, each pedestrian a thought colliding against another. He was a middle-aged man, worn at the edges like an old book but with eyes that burned with a restless energy. Today's burden seemed heavier than usual, much like Hercules' own, when faced with his twelve monumental tasks.

Thomas had recently been tasked with leading a community project to revitalize a neglected neighborhood park—a place that had become more symbolic of decay than recreation. The project felt Herculean not just in its physical scope but also in its underlying social implications: it was about overcoming communal neglect and fostering unity in an area marked by division.

As he passed the park, he paused to survey its overgrown paths and graffiti-tagged benches. Children played near a broken fountain, their laughter echoing off silent statues that watched over unkept lawns. The sight stirred something deep within him—a mixture of dismay and resolve.

He thought about Hercules' battle with the Nemean Lion, drawing parallels between the lion's invincible hide and the seemingly impossible social barriers he faced: poverty, distrust, and apathy. How do you conquer such beasts without weapons or armor? Thomas wondered if community spirit could be his version of Hercules' club.

Interrupting his reverie, an elderly woman approached him hesitantly. "Will there really be flowers here again?" she asked, her voice carrying traces of hope mingled with skepticism. Thomas looked into her eyes and saw reflections of past promises unkept by others before him.

"Yes," he replied firmly, more to convince himself than her. "And benches that aren't just for sitting but for sharing stories and dreams."

Walking home as dusk painted the sky in strokes of orange and purple, Thomas mulled over another Labor — Hercules cleaning the Augean stables. An impossible task made possible by redirecting rivers. Could he, too, find a river to redirect? Could new partnerships be those rivers—bringing fresh energy and washing away years of neglect?

His path took him past small cafes spilling warm light onto sidewalks where couples shared quiet conversations over coffee. The normalcy of their lives contrasted sharply with his tangled thoughts, which wrestled endlessly like those of Hercules and Antaeus.

As night fell and Thomas reached his small apartment overlooking the cityscape—a labyrinth of lights below—he pondered how personal transformation might mirror societal change. Was this project his own Hydra, with each head cut off revealing two more issues requiring attention?

One question lingered as he gazed out across rooftops under starlit skies, contemplating these mythic challenges made manifest in modern trials: In striving to transform our surroundings, might we also transform ourselves?

Unveiling Hercules: More Than Just Myth

When we delve into the tales of Hercules and his Twelve Labors, we uncover layers that resonate deeply with our personal and societal struggles. These stories passed down through the ages are relics of ancient heroics and mirrors reflecting our life challenges. In exploring these narratives, we find a robust framework to understand our adversities and the collective human journey toward overcoming them.

Hercules' legendary exploits go beyond mere physical conquests; they symbolize a quest for personal transformation and societal evolution. Each labor he undertakes represents a fundamental human challenge—fear, persistence, or redemption. By interpreting these myths metaphorically, we can extract valuable lessons applicable to our modern lives. This approach allows us to reconnect with these ancient stories and draw strength from their timeless wisdom.

The symbolic significance of each of Hercules' labors opens up discussions about **personal growth** and **social resilience**. For instance, slaying the Nemean Lion can be seen as overcoming personal fears that paralyze us from moving forward. Similarly, cleaning the Augean stables daily highlights the importance of solving seemingly impossible problems through innovative thinking.

Reflecting on Our Challenges Through Hercules' Tasks

In this chapter, we will explore how these mythological tasks are not just stories but reflections of today's adversities. Each labor carries a story of struggle and triumph that is highly relevant to individual experiences and societal challenges. This exploration will deepen our understanding of Hercules' quests and empower us to tackle our own life's labors with renewed perspective and vigor.

Applying these symbolic meanings to current real-life challenges offers a fresh viewpoint on problem-solving and personal development. Whether dealing with a challenging workplace environment (akin to the capture of the Ceryneian Hind) or navigating personal loss and recovery (echoed in the retrieval of Cerberus), the labors provide a blueprint for resilience and courage.

Applying Ancient Wisdom to Modern Adversities

The tales of Hercules teach us about the virtues of endurance and adaptability, which are essential in today's fast-paced world. By drawing parallels between Hercules' labors and contemporary issues, we learn how ancient wisdom can inform modern coping strategies for overcoming difficulties.

This chapter invites you to journey alongside Hercules, not just as a distant mythical figure but as a reflection of ourselves facing the labors of our own lives. As we dissect these stories, we discover tools for personal empowerment and insights into building stronger communities.

By revisiting these ancient myths through a modern lens, we do more than retell old stories—we breathe new life into them, making them relevant and inspirational for today's challenges. Join us as we unlock the enduring power of these legends and apply their lessons in ways that resonate with our lives now.

Throughout history, Hercules' Twelve Labors have been perceived as monumental tasks of physical strength and endurance. However, when we delve deeper into these ancient tales, we uncover a treasure trove of metaphorical significance that resonates with the personal and societal challenges we face today. Each labor symbolizes a unique human experience, offering valuable insights into perseverance, resilience, and growth. By exploring the symbolic layers of Hercules' trials, we can unlock hidden wisdom that transcends time and culture.

One of the most iconic labors, the slaying of the Nemean Lion, represents **courage** in the face of seemingly insurmountable obstacles. The lion's impenetrable skin mirrors the tough exterior we must break through to conquer our fears and doubts. Just as Hercules faced the fierce beast head-on, we, too, can find the strength within us to confront our inner demons and emerge victorious.

Another labor, capturing the Golden Hind, embodies **persistence and determination**. The elusive nature of the hind symbolizes our relentless pursuit of goals and dreams despite setbacks and challenges. Like Hercules chasing the swift creature through forests and mountains, we must stay focused on our aspirations, never giving up until we achieve our goals.

The cleansing of the Augean Stables is a powerful metaphor for **overcoming obstacles** through **innovative thinking**. Instead of relying solely on brute force, Hercules redirects rivers to clean the filthy stables in a creative solution to a seemingly impossible task. This labor teaches us to think outside the box, approach problems from different angles, and find unconventional ways to surmount difficulties in our own lives.

We discover profound lessons that mirror our personal journeys as we unravel the metaphorical layers of Hercules' Twelve Labors. Each labor offers a unique perspective on human emotions, struggles, and triumphs, inviting us to reflect on our experiences and challenges. By embracing these symbolic meanings, we can find inspiration and guidance in navigating the complexities of life with courage, resilience, and unwavering determination.

Uncover how these ancient tales can illuminate your path forward.

Throughout mythology, we often find reflections of personal and societal challenges that resonate deeply with our own experiences. The trials and tribulations of legendary figures like Hercules can mirror our struggles, offering valuable insights into overcoming adversities. By delving into these ancient tales, we can uncover profound truths about human nature and the obstacles we encounter in our personal and collective journeys.

Mythological Challenges as Personal Adversities: The Twelve Labors of Hercules symbolize individuals' personal hurdles. From battling inner demons to overcoming external obstacles, each labor represents a different facet of the human experience. By understanding these mythological challenges as metaphors for our own struggles, we can gain a fresh perspective on navigating difficulties and emerge stronger on the other side.

Societal Adversities Embedded in Myth: Beyond personal adversities, mythological stories also shed light on broader societal issues that have plagued humanity for centuries. Themes of power struggles, injustice, and moral dilemmas are intricately woven into the fabric of these ancient tales, reflecting the timeless nature of social challenges. By exploring these narratives with a critical eye, we can draw parallels to contemporary issues and gain valuable insights into addressing societal adversities.

Finding Relevance in Ancient Stories: While the myths of Hercules may seem distant and fantastical, their underlying messages are deeply rooted in universal truths that transcend time and culture. By recognizing the parallels between mythological challenges and our realities, we can uncover hidden wisdom that guides us through life's complexities. These ancient stories serve as beacons of hope and resilience, reminding us that we have the strength to persevere even in the face of seemingly insurmountable obstacles.

Empowering Through Reflection: When we take the time to reflect on the personal and societal adversities depicted in mythology, we empower ourselves to confront similar challenges in our own lives. By drawing inspiration from the courage and resilience exhibited by mythological heroes, we can find the inner strength to face our fears, stand up against injustice, and strive for a better world. Through introspection and contemplation of these ancient tales, we unlock a treasure trove of insights that propel us toward personal growth and societal change.

Applying Ancient Wisdom to Modern Challenges: The lessons from mythological stories are not confined to the past but are relevant today. We can navigate complex issues with clarity and determination by applying the symbolic meanings derived from Hercules' tasks to contemporary challenges. Whether grappling with personal setbacks or societal injustices, the wisdom embedded in these ancient myths offers a guiding light that illuminates our path forward.

By recognizing the personal and societal adversities reflected in mythological challenges, we open ourselves up to a wealth of wisdom that transcends time and culture. Through introspection, reflection, and application of these ancient lessons to modern-day struggles, we embark on a transformative journey toward self-discovery and societal evolution. The myths of Hercules serve as poignant reminders that within every challenge lies an opportunity for growth, resilience, and positive change.

Conceptual Model in Systems Theory

The Conceptual Model in Systems Theory provides a structured approach to understanding the interconnectedness between Hercules' Twelve Labors and their implications for personal and societal evolution. This model breaks down Hercules' tasks into distinct components, highlighting inputs, processes, outputs, and outcomes. By examining each labor as a system, we can better grasp the complexity of the challenges Hercules faced and the lessons they offer for modern-day adversities.

Inputs:

Inputs in this model represent the challenges presented in each of Hercules' Twelve Labors. These challenges serve as the starting point for Hercules' journey, symbolizing various personal and societal obstacles individuals encounter. By identifying these challenges as inputs, we can recognize the initial hurdles that must be overcome to achieve growth and transformation.

Processes:

The model's processes detail Hercules' actions to conquer each challenge. These actions include Hercules' strategies, strengths, and virtues displayed during his labors. Understanding these processes allows us to analyze the methods employed to surmount difficulties, offering insights into the resilience, determination, and problem-solving skills necessary for facing real-life challenges.

Outputs:

Outputs signify the immediate results of Hercules' labors. These outcomes showcase the direct consequences of Hercules' actions, such as defeating a monstrous creature or completing a seemingly impossible task. By examining these outputs, readers can witness the tangible impact of overcoming obstacles and the rewards of perseverance and courage.

Outcomes:

Outcomes represent the longer-term effects of Hercules' Twelve Labors on himself and society. They delve into the lasting impacts of personal growth, character development, and cultural influence stemming from Hercules' triumphs. By exploring these outcomes, readers can reflect on how overcoming challenges contributes to individual evolution and shapes collective values and narratives.

By analyzing feedback loops within this model, we can observe how each labor contributes to Hercules' personal growth and broader societal development. The interconnected nature of inputs, processes, outputs, and outcomes showcases how overcoming adversity leads to transformation on both individual and societal levels. Through this system's perspective, readers can draw parallels between Hercules' mythological tasks and contemporary life challenges, fostering a deeper understanding of resilience, perseverance, and growth.

Beyond their narrative thrill, Hercules' Twelve Labors serves as powerful metaphors for our challenges in our personal and societal spheres. Each labor symbolizing a different facet of human struggle offers invaluable lessons on perseverance, courage, and resilience—qualities as relevant today as they were in ancient times.

Step-by-Step Process: "Laboring Towards Enlightenment"

Goal: To utilize the metaphorical lessons of Hercules' Twelve Labors to navigate and overcome personal and societal adversities effectively.

Overview: This process guides you through understanding, connecting, applying, discussing, and finally taking action based on the symbolic meanings of Hercules' challenges. It's designed to transform ancient insights into practical solutions for today's challenges.

1. **Understanding the Metaphorical Significances of Hercules' Twelve Labors**

○ Begin with a thorough reading of each labor, noting Hercules' specific adversities.

○ Reflect on the symbolic meanings and consider their relevance to personal growth and societal issues.

○ Dedicate time to introspect how these stories mirror your life experiences or those around you.

1. **Recognizing Personal and Societal Adversities Reflected in Mythological Challenges**

○ List down current personal and community challenges.

○ Draw parallels between these real-life adversities and Hercules' mythical struggles.

○ Think about Hercules's strategies and how similar approaches can be applied to your challenges.

1. **Applying Symbolic Meanings to Current Real-Life Challenges**

- Select mythological challenges that resonate most with your personal or societal situations.

- Craft reflections or journal entries to explore these connections more deeply.

- Use Hercules' strategies as a model for addressing these modern-day challenges.

1. **Discussing and Sharing Insights**

○ Engage with others exploring similar mythological themes in study groups or online forums.

○ Share your findings and strategies while absorbing different perspectives.

○ Foster a collaborative environment to enhance understanding and discover new approaches.

1. **Taking Action**

○ Identify actionable steps or changes inspired by Hercules' labors that can be implemented in your life or community.

○ Develop a clear plan with specific objectives and timelines to ensure these actions are realized.

○ Share your commitments with peers or mentors to gain support and accountability.

This structured approach deepens your understanding of Hercules' labors. It equips you with the tools to tackle modern challenges with wisdom from these ancient myths. By reflecting on these timeless stories, you can uncover strategies that foster resilience and adaptability in your personal life and community. As we navigate our labors like Hercules, we can emerge more robust and enlightened, ready to face the next challenge with confidence and insight.

Chapter 4: Mythology in Multimedia

In the dim glow of the early morning, Thomas sat by his desk, a stack of weathered books piled high beside his laptop. The faint chirping of birds outside blended with the distant hum of a waking city. He was a scholar, profoundly in the throes of crafting a curriculum that would bring ancient myths to life for his students. The room smelled of old paper and coffee, an aroma that comforted him amidst his scholarly battles.

His eyes scanned through digital pages—videos, podcasts, documentaries—all aimed at unraveling the intricate tapestries of Greek and Norse mythology. Thomas believed in the power of multimedia to transform learning from a passive to an engaging experience. He remembered how dry texts had failed to ignite passion in his younger self, how the myths had seemed like distant, unrelatable tales until he saw them enacted on screen.

As he sifted through resources, Thomas's mind wandered back to a seminar he attended last year, where an animated film on Hercules had left him mesmerized by its vivid portrayal of Herculean trials. The clash of titans on screen had brought an ancient world to life with such vigor that it lingered in his memory. He wanted his students to feel that same thrill—the pulse of ancient drums in their veins as they connected with heroes and gods through more than just words.

He paused as he came across a podcast series featuring discussions by mythologists from around the globe. Each voice offered a new perspective, enriching the narrative with cultural nuances that textbooks often glossed over. It reminded him how mythology could bridge eras and cultures, connecting us through our collective fascination with storytelling.

Interrupting his reverie was the sharp ring of his phone—an old friend calling to discuss their upcoming collaborative project on integrating virtual reality into classical education. As they spoke about potential scenarios where students could virtually step into Achilles' shoes or navigate the labyrinthine world of Minos, Thomas felt a surge of excitement at the prospect.

He hung up and leaned back in his chair, eyes fixed out the window where dawn was breaking into the morning light. Could these technologies genuinely capture the essence of such epic narratives? Could they stir hearts and minds as profoundly as the myths once did?

As he pondered this integration of ancient lore with modern media, Thomas wondered: How far can we stretch these old stories before they lose their magic? Or will these new formats bring us closer than ever to understanding their true spirit?

Unveiling New Realms: How Multimedia Transforms Our Mythological Understanding

In an era where digital media reigns supreme, the ancient tales of Hercules and the Pantheon are finding new life. This revitalization is about retelling old stories and enhancing how we learn and connect with these myths through modern multimedia tools. From the immersive visuals of documentaries to the intimate narratives of podcasts, each medium offers a unique lens through which we can explore these timeless tales.

Multimedia resources have revolutionized educational methodologies across various fields, and mythology is no exception. By integrating videos, podcasts, and interactive platforms into the study of myths, learners gain a multi-sensory experience that often leads to deeper understanding and retention. This chapter will explore how these resources serve not just as tools for entertainment but as powerful educational allies that bring complex mythological themes into more precise focus.

The impact of documentaries on mythology education cannot be overstated. They provide a visual and auditory narrative that can make the abstract elements of myths more tangible and relatable. For example, seeing the landscapes of ancient Greece or visual reenactments of Hercules' labors can transform a textual description into a vivid, memorable encounter. We will delve into how these visual stories complement traditional text-based learning and how they can foster a more nuanced comprehension of mythological themes.

On the other hand, podcasts offer a personal touch through storytelling that engages listeners in a conversational manner. They allow for a deeper dive into topics that might only be brushed upon in books or lectures. By analyzing popular mythology-focused podcasts, this chapter will highlight how the oral tradition of storytelling—so central to the original form of myths—continues to be an effective tool in education today.

Moreover, videos and animated series provide unprecedented accessibility to these stories. They can break down complex narratives into engaging segments that capture the imagination of all age groups. We will evaluate various video formats and discuss their effectiveness in making mythology accessible to a broader audience, including young learners who might find traditional texts less appealing.

Each of these multimedia formats brings its own strengths to learning environments. By combining them, educators and storytellers can create a rich tapestry of educational content that appeals to diverse learning styles and preferences. This chapter aims to provide insights into how effectively these tools can be utilized to educate and inspire new generations about the rich heritage of mythological stories.

In doing so, we reframe these ancient narratives within modern contexts, making them not only more accessible but also more engaging for everyone. By embracing multimedia as a critical component in the study of mythology, we open up new pathways for exploration and understanding that were unimaginable in the past. This approach does not replace traditional methods but enriches them. It offers multiple perspectives and deeper connections to the legendary tales that have shaped human culture for millennia.

Thus, as we journey through this exploration of multimedia in mythology education, we invite readers to discover how ancient stories can be transformed by modern technology—not losing their essence but unfolding their depth in ways that resonate with today's audiences.

In today's digital age, integrating multimedia resources has revolutionized how we learn about mythology. **Podcasts, videos, documentaries**, and various online platforms have made ancient myths more accessible and engaging. These multimedia tools offer a dynamic approach to exploring mythological themes, providing diverse perspectives, and enhancing the learning experience. By incorporating visual and auditory elements, learners can immerse themselves in the captivating narratives of gods, heroes, and mythical creatures.

One significant advantage of multimedia resources is their ability to demystify complex mythological concepts. Through engaging visuals and expert commentary, these tools break down intricate stories into digestible segments, making them easier to understand and remember. By presenting myths in a more relatable and interactive format, learners can grasp the underlying themes and moral lessons embedded within these ancient tales.

Moreover, multimedia resources bring mythology to life by appealing to multiple senses. Videos and documentaries narrate the stories and showcase stunning visuals, sound effects, and music that create a rich sensory experience. This immersive approach captivates the audience and fosters a deeper connection with the mythical world, making the narratives more vivid and memorable.

Another critical benefit of multimedia in learning mythology is the opportunity for a more comprehensive exploration of different cultural perspectives. Podcasts featuring scholars from various backgrounds, documentaries on global mythologies, and online videos showcasing diverse interpretations all contribute to a more nuanced understanding of myths across civilizations. This exposure to a wide range of viewpoints enriches the learning process. It encourages critical thinking about how myths have shaped societies throughout history.

By embracing multimedia resources in the study of mythology, learners can engage with these timeless tales in a modern and dynamic way. The combination of visuals, audio, expert insights, and interactive content offers a holistic learning experience that transcends traditional methods.

Whether through podcasts that delve deep into specific myths or videos that visualize epic battles between gods and monsters, multimedia resources provide an exciting avenue for exploring the rich tapestry of mythological storytelling.

Continue reading to discover how documentaries, podcasts, and videos can enhance your understanding of mythological themes.

In today's digital age, multimedia resources such as documentaries, podcasts, and videos enhance our understanding of mythological themes. These dynamic mediums offer a multi-sensory experience that can bring ancient stories to life in ways that traditional text alone cannot achieve. **These formats provide a more immersive and captivating exploration of mythology by incorporating visuals, sound effects, expert commentary, and engaging storytelling.**

Documentaries serve as valuable tools for delving deep into myths' historical and cultural contexts. Through interviews with scholars, visits to archaeological sites, and stunning visuals, documentaries offer a comprehensive look at the significance of these ancient tales. **The combination of visuals and expert analysis helps viewers gain a nuanced understanding of the myths' relevance and enduring impact on society.**

On the other hand, podcasts offer a more intimate and conversational approach to exploring mythology. **Listening to podcasts allows a deep dive into specific themes or characters**, often presented in an engaging narrative format. **The audio medium stimulates the imagination**, painting vivid mental pictures that can resonate with listeners on a personal level. Podcasts often feature discussions among experts or enthusiasts, providing diverse perspectives and insights into mythological interpretations.

Regarding **videos**, platforms like YouTube have become treasure troves of mythological content. **From animated retellings of classic myths to educational videos breaking down complex themes**, a wide range of content is available for every level of interest and expertise. **Visual aids can aid comprehension**, making abstract concepts more tangible and accessible.

These multimedia resources are powerful tools for anyone looking to deepen their understanding of mythology. **They offer diverse perspectives, engage multiple senses, and cater to various learning styles**. Whether you prefer visually stunning documentaries, thought-provoking podcasts, or visually engaging videos, there is something out there for everyone eager to unravel the mysteries of ancient myths. Embrace these multimedia formats as companions in your mythological journey, enriching your knowledge and appreciation for these timeless tales.

In evaluating the effectiveness of different media formats in making mythology accessible and engaging, it becomes evident that each medium brings a unique dimension to the storytelling experience. **Podcasts**, for instance, offer an auditory journey through myths, allowing listeners to immerse themselves in the tales while going about their daily activities. The convenience of podcasts enables individuals to learn about mythology during commutes, workouts, or downtime, making it a versatile and accessible option for busy modern lifestyles.

Conversely, videos provide a visual feast for learners, bringing the characters and settings of myths to life in a captivating manner. Watching these stories unfold on screen can enhance comprehension by offering a vivid portrayal of events that might be challenging to imagine solely through text. Visual cues and cinematic techniques can evoke emotions and create a more profound connection to the mythological narratives.

Documentaries stand out as educational tools that combine visual storytelling with in-depth analysis and expert commentary. These films delve into the historical context, symbolism, and cultural significance of myths, providing viewers with a comprehensive understanding of the stories' relevance. Documentaries offer entertainment and education, making them valuable resources for those seeking a deeper exploration of mythology.

By incorporating various multimedia elements into the learning process, individuals can engage with mythology on multiple levels, catering to different learning preferences and styles. **Interactive websites**, for instance, offer an immersive experience where users can navigate through interactive maps, quizzes, and multimedia content to deepen their understanding of myths. This dynamic approach encourages active participation and exploration, fostering a sense of discovery and curiosity.

Virtual reality (VR) experiences represent the cutting edge of multimedia technology in mythological education. By donning a VR headset, learners can step into the world of ancient myths, interact with legendary figures, and explore mythical realms firsthand. This innovative approach enhances engagement by providing a sensory-rich environment that stimulates imagination and creates lasting impressions.

In conclusion, today's diverse multimedia formats presents exciting opportunities to make mythology more accessible and engaging than ever before. Whether through podcasts for on-the-go learning, videos for visual immersion, documentaries for comprehensive insights, interactive websites for hands-on exploration, or VR experiences for immersive journeys, each medium offers a unique way to connect with ancient stories. By embracing these multimedia tools, individuals can unlock the power of mythology in new and transformative ways.

The dynamic interplay between mythology and multimedia is not just a modern phenomenon but a profound expansion of how we connect with these age-old stories. By integrating documentaries, podcasts, and videos into exploring myths, we unlock new dimensions of understanding and engagement. This method not only makes learning more accessible but also more compelling, ensuring that the rich tapestry of mythological themes resonates with a diverse, contemporary audience.

The effectiveness of multimedia in teaching mythology lies in its ability to **bring stories to life**.

Visual and auditory elements complement the textual narratives, providing a fuller, more immersive experience. For example, hearing the thunderous roar in a podcast about Zeus or watching the vibrant reenactments of Hercules' labors in a documentary can transform abstract readings into tangible, memorable events. This sensory enhancement aids in deeper retention and appreciation of the material.

Moreover, these varied formats cater to different learning styles and preferences, making mythology **accessible to a broader range of learners**. Whether a visual learner excited by videos or an auditory learner captivated by podcasts, multimedia opens up multiple pathways for engagement. This inclusivity is crucial in educational settings, where the goal is to reach and inspire every student.

Reflecting on the journey through this chapter, it becomes clear that multimedia is not just an adjunct but a powerful tool in the education of mythology. It offers a bridge between ancient narratives and modern technology, fostering an informative and inspiring learning environment. As we explore Hercules and the Pantheon, let us continue to embrace these innovative tools that breathe new life into old legends, making them relevant and exhilarating for today's audience.

By harnessing the potential of multimedia resources, we are preserving these timeless stories and passing on their wisdom and wonder to future generations. Let's carry this enthusiasm and curiosity into the remaining chapters, exploring even more ways to delve into the mysteries and marvels of mythology.

Chapter 5: The Power of Community in Myth-Making

Elena walked through the university campus in the soft twilight of an early spring evening, her mind a hive of buzzing thoughts. She was a professor of comparative mythology, and today, she is pivotal; she launched an online platform dedicated to the interactive study of ancient myths. The air was crisp, carrying the scent of blooming magnolias that lined the path toward the old library. In this place, she often found solace.

Elena stopped momentarily, leaning against the cool stone wall of the library. She remembered how her students had animatedly debated the character of Odysseus in their new digital forum earlier that day. The discussion wasn't just academic; it was personal, each student weaving their own life's threads into the ancient narrative, finding meaning and perhaps guidance in these age-old tales.

Across from her, two students sat on a worn wooden bench, their heads close together over a shared notebook. Their voices were low but excited as they connected mythic themes with modern-day issues—justice, leadership, and morality. Elena smiled faintly; this was precisely what she hoped to achieve—a community learning about myths and living through them.

The bell in the old university tower rang sharply, pulling Elena from her reverie. She started walking again, her steps echoing softly on the cobblestone path. She thought about tomorrow's class, where they would use virtual reality to explore the mythical landscapes of Hades and Olympus. How would experiencing these worlds change their understanding of Persephone's descent or Prometheus' sacrifice?

Just then, a cold gust swept through the campus, rustling papers and whispering through the trees like spirits discussing their next move in hushed tones. It reminded Elena that while technology could bring these stories to life in new ways, it was ultimately up to her and her students to keep their meanings alive and relevant.

As she reached her office and turned on the light, casting a warm glow against the gathering darkness outside, she pondered whether this blend of ancient myth with modern technology could truly bridge time's vast expanse. Could these stories from millennia ago still offer wisdom for today's digital age? What happens when an age-old tale meets a modern mind ready to debate its intricacies?

Unleashing the Collective Force of Myths

The study of mythology, particularly the captivating tales of Hercules and the Pantheon, offers more than just a passage into ancient narratives; it presents a dynamic avenue to foster community, stimulate engaging discussions, and enhance collective understanding. In this chapter, we will delve into the significance of interactive and communal learning platforms and explore how these environments enrich individual knowledge and solidify a community's role in maintaining the vibrancy and relevance of these age-old stories.

The Catalyst of Interactive Learning

Interactive learning platforms serve as a catalyst for deeper comprehension and engagement with mythology. By participating in courses requiring active involvement, learners are not merely recipients of information but also contributors to the learning process. This **active participation** is crucial as it encourages learners to question and connect with the material personally, paving the path for a more profound appreciation of the myths.

Discussion Groups as Arenas for Debate

Engaging in discussion groups offers a unique opportunity to explore the nuances of mythological content. These forums are not just about sharing knowledge but are pivotal in fostering critical thinking and debate. Every interpretation or opinion opens the door to further exploration and understanding, allowing myths to be seen in a new light. The exchange of ideas in such groups ensures that learning is not a solitary journey but a communal experience that enriches everyone involved.

Building a Vibrant Mythological Community

The power of community in myth-making cannot be overstated. By fostering a group of enthusiastic learners, these platforms ensure that mythology remains a living tradition rather than a mere historical recount. This community does not just consume stories; it breathes life into them, allowing Hercules and his fellow deities to transcend the confines of ancient texts and become relevant in modern discussions about morality, heroism, and human nature.

Interactive platforms and discussion groups do more than educate; they connect individuals from diverse backgrounds through their shared love for mythology. This connection builds a supportive network where members motivate each other to explore deeper and understand better. The sense of belonging from being part of such a group can significantly enhance the learning experience.

As we progress through this exploration, remember that your engagement with these platforms is not just about acquiring knowledge; it's about being part \textit{of} something more significant—a community that actively shapes how these timeless tales are perceived and valued across generations.

Embrace Your Role in Mythology Today

Encouragingly, every discussion you engage in and every insight you share contributes to this vibrant tapestry of mythology. Your participation is pivotal in ensuring these stories are not lost but continue inspiring, teaching, and provoking thought among contemporary audiences.

Thus, as we navigate through this chapter, consider how your involvement on these platforms can transform your understanding and how these ancient narratives continue to resonate today.

Interactive and communal learning platforms provide a dynamic space for exploring mythology in a new light. These platforms offer a unique opportunity to engage with ancient stories in a way that goes beyond traditional methods. Participating in interactive courses or joining discussion groups focused on mythology allows learners to delve deeper into the narratives, question their meanings, and share interpretations with others. This collaborative approach enriches individual understanding and fosters a sense of community around these timeless tales.

Participants can bring their diverse perspectives to the table in these interactive settings, creating a rich tapestry of interpretations and insights. **Sharing ideas** and engaging in discussions with fellow enthusiasts can lead to new discoveries and revelations about mythological stories. The communal aspect of these platforms encourages **critical thinking**. It challenges individuals to explore the nuances of the narratives, uncovering layers of meaning that may have been previously overlooked.

Moreover, being part of a community passionate about mythology can be incredibly rewarding. **Connecting** with like-minded individuals who are fascinated by ancient tales creates a sense of belonging and camaraderie. By exchanging thoughts and interpretations, participants deepen their own understanding and contribute to the collective knowledge of the group. This collaborative effort ensures that mythological stories remain relevant and vibrant in today's world.

Through interactive and communal learning platforms, learners can actively engage with mythology, moving beyond passive consumption to become co-creators of meaning. By participating in discussions, debates, and shared exploration of ancient narratives, individuals can develop a deeper appreciation for the richness and complexity of mythological tales. This active involvement enhances personal growth and contributes to the preservation and evolution of these timeless stories.

Dive deeper into the power of community engagement in myth-making.

Engage in discussion groups and courses encouraging critical thinking and debate on mythological content.

Interactive learning platforms offer a unique opportunity to delve deep into mythology. By participating in discussion groups and courses focused on ancient tales, individuals can absorb the stories and actively engage with them. These platforms provide a space where questions are encouraged, interpretations are debated, and **knowledge is collectively built**. Instead of passively consuming information, learners actively explore myths, allowing for a richer and more profound understanding of these narratives.

Engaging in discussions can help individuals gain new perspectives and insights into mythological stories. Debating different interpretations fosters critical thinking skills and encourages learners to question traditional beliefs. By challenging assumptions and exploring alternative viewpoints, participants can uncover hidden meanings within myths and **develop a deeper connection** to the stories and characters.

Participating in courses encouraging debate on mythological content can be intellectually stimulating and emotionally rewarding. Gripping at complex themes and moral dilemmas presented in ancient tales can lead to personal growth and self-discovery. Confronting challenging topics within mythology allows individuals to reflect on their values and beliefs, **ultimately leading to greater self-awareness.**

Being part of a community passionate about mythology can be incredibly enriching. Engaging in discussions with like-minded individuals who appreciate the depth and complexity of ancient stories can foster a sense of belonging and camaraderie. Participants can learn from each other's perspectives, **expand their knowledge**, and forge lasting connections with fellow enthusiasts through these interactions.

Discussion groups and courses provide a platform for individuals to learn about mythology and contribute to its ongoing relevance. Learners play a crucial role in keeping these ancient narratives alive and vibrant by actively participating in discussions, sharing insights, and debating interpretations. Through their engagement, they contribute to the evolution of mythological understanding **and ensure that these stories resonate with future generations.**

In conclusion, engaging in discussion groups and courses focused on mythological content offers a dynamic and interactive way to explore ancient tales. By fostering critical thinking, encouraging debate, and building a sense of community, these platforms provide an enriching experience that goes beyond passive learning. Through active participation and thoughtful engagement with mythology, individuals can deepen their understanding of these timeless stories and **contribute to their enduring relevance.**

Building a community around the exploration of mythological stories is a powerful way to keep these ancient narratives alive and relevant. By fostering a space where individuals can share interpretations, ask questions, and engage in discussions, the richness of mythology can be continually uncovered and appreciated. **Community engagement deepens individual understanding and contributes to the collective wisdom of all participants.**

Through interactive platforms like online forums, study groups, or discussion circles, enthusiasts can come together to delve into the layers of meaning within mythological tales. **These communal spaces** provide a supportive environment for learners to challenge assumptions, spark debates, and offer fresh perspectives on age-old stories.

In such communities, diverse viewpoints merge to create a tapestry of interpretations that breathe new life into ancient myths. **By sharing insights and reflections with others, individuals can expand their own understanding while enriching their peers' experiences.**

The collaborative nature of these interactions nurtures a sense of belonging and shared purpose among members, fostering a deeper connection to the stories and the community around them. As participants engage in lively debates and contemplative conversations, they contribute to a dynamic exchange of ideas that keeps mythology vibrant and evolving.

By actively participating in these communal spaces, individuals become not just consumers but creators of mythological knowledge. **Their contributions help shape the ongoing dialogue surrounding these narratives,** ensuring they remain relevant and meaningful in contemporary times.

As individuals share their unique perspectives and insights within a community dedicated to mythological exploration, they deepen their understanding and inspire others to see these ancient stories in a new light. **The power of community lies in its ability to transform passive observers into active participants,** each contributing its piece to the ever-evolving tapestry of myth.

The profound impact of community involvement in the study and perpetuation of mythology cannot be overstressed. We tap into a rich reservoir of collective intelligence and experience by engaging with interactive and communal learning platforms. This approach deepens individual understanding and breathes new life into ancient narratives, ensuring they remain relevant and vibrant in our modern world.

Interactive platforms and discussion groups serve as the crucibles where the old stories of Hercules and the Pantheon are not just retold but reimagined and scrutinized. Here, every participant becomes a student and a teacher, contributing unique perspectives and enriching the group's collective insight. This dynamic environment encourages critical thinking and robust debates, fostering a deeper connection with the material that solitary study seldom offers.

Moreover, we ensure their continual evolution by fostering a community around these mythological tales. As new interpretations and ideas emerge, these stories do not remain static; they grow with us, reflecting contemporary values and questions. This communal contribution is vital for keeping mythology alive and pertinent across generations.

Reflecting on our journey through this chapter, it is clear that the power of community in myth-making is not just about preserving stories but transforming them into living dialogues that continue to inspire and challenge us. Each discussion and shared story adds layers to our understanding and keeps the ancient world accessible and relevant to modern society.

Let us then continue to nurture these communal spaces of learning. Let us keep the legends of Hercules and his fellow deities vibrant as we carry their tales forward with renewed meaning and vitality. The task is as noble as it is rewarding—ensuring that these time-honored myths continue to enlighten, entertain, and educate us all.

Chapter 6: Reflecting Through Myths

In the heart of Athens, where modernity brushes against the ancient stones, Thomas walked through the bustling Syntagma Square, his thoughts as crowded as the people around him. He was a professor of philosophy, and lately, his lectures had been infiltrated by the rich tapestry of Greek mythology. Today was no exception; he was pondering how these myths' moral complexities could be applied to contemporary ethical dilemmas.

As he passed a group of tourists snapping photos of the Parliament building, his mind drifted to the myth of Prometheus – the Titan who defied Zeus to bring fire to humanity. Thomas mulled over Prometheus's punishment for his defiance, bound to have his liver pecked out each day only for it to regenerate each night. "Is civil disobedience still as necessary today?" he wondered silently. "Are there still fires that need stealing in our world?"

The scent of fresh souvlaki from a nearby vendor pulled him back from ancient times to present reality. He noticed a young boy tugging at his mother's hand, eagerly pointing at the food stand. The simple scene reminded him of Demeter and Persephone—a tale of deep maternal love and the cycles of nature that resonate with every sown seed and harvested crop.

Further along, as he strolled near the National Garden, Thomas stopped to watch an older man gently tending to a bed of marigolds. The gardener's careful attention to each plant seemed almost ritualistic, echoing ancient rites and offerings. It struck Thomas how myths could serve as stories and frameworks for understanding life's deeper rhythms and human connections.

The rustling leaves above whispered like muses inspiring him; they stirred questions about how these old narratives could inform our understanding of nature and our role. Could understanding Hades' cold dominion over the underworld help society address its views on death or loss?

As dusk painted shadows on stone paths, Thomas's reflections gathered like clouds before a storm. Each step seemed synced with a turn in his thoughts—from heroism in myths urging one towards more significant personal growth to their warnings about hubris leading one astray.

He paused before an ancient olive tree near the garden's exit; its gnarled trunk bore witness to countless suns rising and setting—much like Sisyphus's eternal struggle up that hill. Past and present seemed not so distant after all, and at this moment, it was suspended between day and night.

By delving into these age-old stories, we might find solace and solutions for modern-day challenges.

Unraveling the Threads of Time: How Myths Shape Our Reality

Mythology, often seen as a collection of quaint stories from our ancestors, holds transformative power that extends far beyond ancient narratives. In the realm of Hercules and the Pantheon, myths are not just tales of heroism and divine intrigue but are reflections of human nature and societal values that resonate through the ages. This chapter embarks on a profound exploration of how **regular reflection** on these mythological themes can catalyze **personal growth** and a deeper understanding of contemporary societal dilemmas.

The Mirror of Mythology

When we delve into the stories of Hercules' labors or the intricate affairs of the gods, we are not merely entertaining ourselves with tales of a bygone era. Instead, we engage in a process that mirrors our own lives back to us, offering insights into our personal and collective psyche. By reflecting on these age-old tales, we uncover layers of meaning that relate directly to our own experiences and challenges. This reflective practice is not just an academic exercise but a **journey toward self-discovery** and empowerment.

Ethics and Morals from Antiquity

The ethical dilemmas and moral questions that pervade these ancient stories are startlingly relevant today. Consider Hercules' choices and consequences; these narratives compel us to reflect on our values and the ramifications of our actions in modern contexts. This chapter discusses how applying mythological morals to **contemporary issues** such as justice, leadership, and integrity can illuminate new pathways for societal advancement and personal accountability.

Cultivating Cultural and Metaphysical Insights

Beyond personal reflection, engaging deeply with myths enhances our understanding of different cultures and their worldviews. This enriched perspective fosters greater empathy and multicultural awareness, which is crucial in today's globalized society. Moreover, by exploring metaphysical themes within these legends—such as fate versus free will or the nature of the divine—we open ourselves to broader existential discussions that can profoundly shape our worldview.

Thus, regularly engaging with mythology becomes an enriching educational tool, one that promotes not only personal insight but also cultural literacy. As we traverse these legendary narratives, we do more than revisit old tales; we activate a powerful framework for understanding the fabric of human existence across different epochs.

Through this exploration, this chapter aims to inspire readers to see Hercules not just as a mythical hero but as a symbol whose struggles and triumphs can inform our own life choices. The stories of the Pantheon are not static; they evolve with us, offering fresh insights and guidance as we navigate our complex world.

By fostering a habit of mythological reflection, we do not escape reality; instead, we penetrate deeper into its essence, equipped with timeless wisdom distilled through centuries. Engage actively with these stories; let them challenge, change, and fortify you as you reflect on your journey through life mirrored in the heroic quests and divine dramas of the old.

Reflection on mythological themes is a powerful tool for personal growth and understanding. By delving into the stories of gods and heroes from ancient civilizations, we can uncover profound insights that resonate with our own lives. These myths often pose moral dilemmas, ethical questions, and existential quandaries that have stood the test of time. **Regularly engaging with these timeless tales allows us to explore our values, beliefs, and behaviors more deeply and meaningfully.**

As we reflect on the trials and triumphs of mythological characters, we are prompted to consider our own actions and choices. The struggles of Hercules against impossible tasks, the wisdom of Athena in times of conflict, or the hubris of Icarus soaring too close to the sun—all these narratives offer mirrors through which we can examine our strengths and weaknesses. **Through this introspection, we gain clarity about our motivations, fears, and aspirations**, leading to personal growth and self-awareness.

Mythological themes also provide a rich tapestry for exploring universal truths and timeless lessons. Whether it's the consequences of greed, the importance of courage in the face of adversity, or the power of love to overcome obstacles, myths offer a treasure trove of wisdom waiting to be uncovered. **By reflecting on these themes**, we can extract valuable insights that can guide us in navigating the complexities of modern life.

Moreover, engaging with mythological narratives fosters empathy and understanding. By imagining ourselves as mythic figures facing monumental challenges, we develop a greater sense of compassion for others grappling with their own struggles. **This empathy extends beyond individual interactions to societal issues** as we see parallels between the moral dilemmas presented in myths and the ethical quandaries confronting our communities today.

In essence, regular reflection on mythological themes is not just an intellectual exercise; it is a transformative practice that can enrich our lives profoundly. **By immersing ourselves in these ancient stories**, we open ourselves to new perspectives, deeper insights, and greater self-awareness. Through this process of reflection, we embark on a journey of self-discovery that can lead to personal growth, enhanced understanding, and a more profound connection to the world around us.

Continue exploring how mythological morals can shed light on contemporary societal issues.

Reflecting on mythological morals and ethical dilemmas can offer valuable insights into contemporary societal issues. By examining the timeless dilemmas presented in ancient myths, we can draw parallels to today's challenges. **The stories of gods and heroes often tackle fundamental questions about human nature, power dynamics, and moral choices,** providing a rich tapestry of narratives that resonate across time.

One key benefit of applying mythological themes to modern society is the opportunity for deep introspection. By pondering the ethical quandaries mythological figures face, we can reflect on our values and beliefs. **For example, considering the consequences of hubris, as seen in the downfall of characters like Icarus or Narcissus,** we may contemplate how pride and arrogance can lead to personal ruin in our own lives or in the leaders of our time.

Moreover, myths offer a lens through which to analyze complex social issues. The power struggles, the quest for justice, and the clash between good and evil portrayed in myths mirror contemporary societal challenges. **By examining how these themes play out in**

myths, we can better understand current events and cultural phenomena.

For instance, exploring the theme of betrayal in stories like that of Judas or Medea can shed light on contemporary issues of trust and loyalty in interpersonal relationships and politics.

Another compelling aspect of applying mythological morals to modern society is the potential for fostering empathy and compassion. By immersing ourselves in the tales of characters facing moral dilemmas, **we can better understand human frailty and complexity. This understanding can lead to more tolerant and inclusive attitudes toward others** as we recognize the universal struggles depicted in myths reflected in our lives and those around us.

Furthermore, engaging with mythological ethics can inspire us to take action toward positive change in our communities. Stories of heroes standing up against injustice or sacrificing their own desires for the greater good can serve as powerful motivators for social activism. **By drawing parallels between the heroic deeds of mythological figures and real-life acts of courage,** we can find inspiration to contribute meaningfully to creating a better world for all.

In conclusion, by delving into the moral quandaries presented in myths and relating them to contemporary societal issues, we open ourselves to a wealth of wisdom and insight that can guide us toward personal growth and social transformation.

The timeless themes found in mythology continue to be relevant today, offering us a deeper understanding of ourselves and a roadmap for navigating the complexities of our ever-evolving world.

Cultivating a deeper understanding of metaphysical concepts and cultural insights through active engagement with myths can be a transformative journey. By delving into the rich tapestry of ancient stories and legends, we open ourselves to profound wisdom and timeless truths that resonate across the ages. **Through reflection and**

contemplation, we can extract valuable lessons that enrich our personal lives and offer a unique perspective on the world around us.

Engaging with myths is akin to deciphering a cryptic code that holds the secrets of human nature, morality, and existence. These tales serve as mirrors reflecting our innermost struggles, desires, and aspirations. By immersing ourselves in the narratives of gods and heroes, we are invited to explore the complexities of the human experience in a way that is both enlightening and empowering.

As we unravel the layers of mythological stories, we begin to unravel the layers of our consciousness. Each myth presents a puzzle waiting to be solved, a riddle challenging us to look beyond the surface and delve into the depths of meaning. Through this process of interpretation and introspection, we gain insight into ourselves and develop a heightened sensitivity to the cultural nuances embedded in these ancient tales.

By actively engaging with myths, we participate in an ongoing dialogue with humanity's collective wisdom. These stories have endured for centuries because they speak to universal truths that transcend time and place. As we immerse ourselves in this timeless narrative tapestry, we become part of a larger conversation about what it means to be human and how we can navigate the complexities of existence with grace and integrity.

The journey into mythology is not just an intellectual exercise but a soul-stirring exploration that awakens our imagination and ignites our sense of wonder. Through these ancient myths, we tap into a wellspring of creativity and inspiration that can fuel our own personal growth and self-discovery. Walking alongside gods and monsters, heroes and villains, we uncover hidden aspects of ourselves that have long been dormant or overlooked.

Embracing myths as more than mere stories but as profound allegories for life allows us to approach them with reverence and curiosity. Each myth offers a unique lens through which to view our reality, challenging us to question our assumptions, confront our fears, and embrace our potential for transformation. In this way, **we become active participants** in the ongoing evolution of these timeless tales, breathing new life into age-old narratives through our own interpretations and reflections.

Through this process, we deepen our metaphysical literacy and cultivate a greater appreciation for the diversity of human experience and belief systems. Myths from different cultures provide us with windows into worlds similar to and vastly different from our own, expanding our capacity for empathy, understanding, and interconnectedness. By embracing the diversity of mythological traditions, we enrich our cultural awareness and foster a more inclusive worldview that honors the richness of human imagination throughout history.

In essence, **active engagement with myths** offers us a roadmap to navigate the complexities of life with wisdom and grace. By reflecting on these timeless tales, we embark on a journey of self-discovery that leads us to profound insights about ourselves, our society, and the world at large. As we delve deeper into the mysteries contained within these ancient narratives, we unlock hidden truths that can transform not only our individual lives but also the collective consciousness of humanity.

Mythical Reflections: A Practical Guide

Regular personal reflection on mythological themes offers profound personal and social benefits. Through this practice, we can uncover insights that apply to today's challenges and enrich our cultural understanding.

Step 1: Practicing Regular Reflection on Mythological Themes

Set aside a specific time each week to immerse yourself in the world of myths. Create a peaceful space where distractions fade, allowing for deep contemplation. Use guiding questions related to the myths you've explored to effectively steer your reflections.

Step 2: Enhancing Personal Growth and Understanding

Identify connections between the moral lessons from myths and today's ethical dilemmas. Apply these ancient stories to your personal decisions and societal viewpoints, challenging and refining your values and beliefs.

Step 3: Engaging with Myths through Active Engagement

Actively seek out cultural activities that celebrate and interpret myths, such as theatrical performances or art exhibitions. Engage in community discussions and workshops that foster a deeper understanding of these stories. Share your interpretations, enhancing communal knowledge and appreciation of mythology.

Step 4: Applying Mythological Morals to Real-Life Situations

Choose contemporary issues that resonate with you and reflect on how mythological morals can inform your approach to these challenges. Develop actionable plans to implement these lessons in both personal actions and community involvement.

Step 5: Cultivating Metaphysical Literacy and Cultural Insights

Expand your knowledge by exploring additional resources that delve into the myths' cultural and historical contexts. Understand the symbolism used in these stories to fully appreciate their deeper meanings. Share these insights, contributing to a richer collective understanding of our cultural heritage.

This step-by-step guide structures our engagement with myths. It ensures that the insights gained are deeply integrated into our lives and communities. Following this path fosters a richer, more connected understanding of the timeless lessons that myths teach us, enhancing personal growth and societal cohesion.

Chapter 7: Divinity and Humanity: The Hercules Complex

In a late afternoon's soft, diffused light, Thomas walked through the grove of ancient olive trees, their gnarled trunks standing as silent witnesses to centuries. The rustle of leaves whispered above him, a gentle sound that seemed to carry the weight of old myths. Thomas, a scholar of classical antiquities, was in Greece on a fellowship to study the enduring impact of mythical heroes on modern ethics. Today, he found himself drawn not to his books but to the land itself.

As he wandered, his mind turned over the myth of Hercules—a divine and mortal figure—and its relevance to his own life's tensions. Thomas had always felt caught between two worlds: the academic aspirations instilled by his scholarly family and the simpler, more immediate life that often tempted him from quieter corners of his world. Like Hercules, who performed feats for immortality while suffering profoundly human pains and passions, Thomas wrestled with these competing natures.

The scent of earth mingled with the saltiness carried inland from the Aegean Sea, grounding him as he pondered Hercules' labors. Each labor was not just a quest but a confrontation between what Hercules was and what he ought to be—an echo of every human's battle between base instincts and higher ethical goals.

Pausing beside an olive tree older than any living human, Thomas touched its bark lightly with his fingertips. He thought about Hercules' second labor—the slaying of the Hydra. Each head cut off had sprouted two more—a metaphor not lost on him for moral dilemmas where every solved issue seemed only to complicate matters further.

A child ran laughing past him suddenly toward a woman calling out in Greek, her voice rich with warmth but commanding attention. The scene pulled Thomas back from ancient times to present realities, reminding him how every personal battle was layered within broader social and historical contexts.

As he resumed walking, his steps crunching softly on a carpet of fallen leaves and twigs underfoot, Thomas considered how Hercules' narrative provided insights into individual moral conflicts and a framework for understanding collective human struggles. How does one balance personal desires against societal expectations? How does one choose which virtues define one's character?

He looked up as the sun descended behind the hills, casting long shadows across his path and painting the sky in strokes of orange and pink. What would it mean for us today if we saw our ethical struggles as Herculean labors—not battles to be won or lost but journeys toward understanding our complex natures?

The Tug of War Within: Exploring the Duality of Hercules

The legendary figure of Hercules, a demigod torn between his divine heritage and human frailties, offers a fascinating mirror of the human condition. This chapter delves into the intriguing dichotomy of Hercules' existence as a sacred entity and a mortal man, grappling with his instincts and ethical dilemmas. His story is a series of mythological feats and a profound narrative reflecting our struggles with morality and virtue.

Hercules' dual nature uniquely positions him as an archetype that understands the broader implications of human moral conflicts. Through his battles, both physical and spiritual, we gain insights into the internal conflicts that define the human experience. Each labor he undertakes is a quest and a chapter in the larger story of navigating between base instincts and noble aspirations.

The Struggle Between Godly Power and Human Weakness

His constant battle with his identity is at the heart of Hercules' narrative. Born of Zeus, yet raised among mortals, Hercules embodies the potent mix of divine power shadowed by human vulnerability. This duality is not just a personal trial but resonates with each of us as we face our daily trials. Analyzing Hercules' life provides a framework to explore how this blend of divinity and mortality influences decisions and actions in the face of moral challenges.

The implications of Hercules' dual nature extend beyond personal introspection; they offer a broader understanding of humanity's universal moral conflicts. By examining how Hercules navigates his path, torn between his godlike strength and mortal emotions, we can better comprehend the complexities that come with our own powers and passions.

Reflecting on Our Own Moral Battles

Hercules' story also prompts us to reflect on our personal journeys through its vivid depiction of his trials. Each labor he undertakes symbolizes more profound philosophical questions about duty, justice, courage, and restraint—themes that resonate deeply within our lives as we strive to balance our desires with our responsibilities.

As we read this chapter, we will explore how these themes play out in Hercules's life and what they teach us about handling our inner conflicts. The aim is not only to understand Hercules as a character but also to use his life as a lens through which we can view our struggles.

This exploration into Hercules' life illuminates the mythological dimensions of his existence and offers practical reflections for our personal growth. Understanding his struggles with his dual nature allows us to gain insights into our battles between primal desires and higher ethical goals.

In this journey through Hercules' tale, let us find inspiration in his strength and wisdom in his weaknesses. As we reflect on these age-old stories, they shed light on modern dilemmas, guiding us toward a more reflective understanding of what it means to be truly human—flawed yet constantly striving for something greater than ourselves.

Hercules, the legendary hero of Greek mythology, embodies a unique struggle with his dual nature as both divine and mortal. This internal conflict is a central theme in his story, reflecting the eternal battle between base instincts and higher ethical aspirations that many individuals face. As a demigod, Hercules possesses incredible strength and power. Yet, he is also subject to the same weaknesses and flaws as any mortal. This duality creates a complex character torn between his divine lineage and the limitations of human existence.

Hercules' divine heritage sets him apart from ordinary humans, giving him extraordinary abilities and a sense of destiny. However, his mortal side grounds him in the reality of pain, suffering, and mortality. This juxtaposition of strengths and vulnerabilities shapes Hercules' journey as he navigates the challenges presented by his godly powers and human frailties. Through this struggle, Hercules grapples with questions of identity, purpose, and morality, mirroring the universal conflicts within the human psyche.

The clash between Hercules' divine and mortal aspects is a metaphor for the broader human experience. His story invites us to contemplate our inner conflicts, the tug-of-war between our higher ideals and primal instincts. Like Hercules, we often find ourselves at odds with conflicting desires and impulses, striving to reconcile our noble aspirations with more base inclinations. This ongoing battle shapes our decisions and actions and ultimately defines our character.

Throughout his adventures, **Hercules confronts various trials** that test his resolve and challenge him to rise above his dual nature. Whether facing mythical beasts or navigating treacherous obstacles, he must draw upon his godly strength and human ingenuity to overcome these obstacles. In doing so, Hercules demonstrates the potential for growth and transformation that comes from embracing all aspects of oneself, even those that seem contradictory.

As readers delve into Hercules' narrative, they are encouraged to reflect on their internal struggles **between their divine aspirations -** their highest values and noblest goals - and their mortal shortcomings - their weaknesses and imperfections. By examining Hercules' journey through this lens, individuals can gain insight into their moral dilemmas and existential conflicts. The hero's story becomes a mirror through which readers can explore their complexities and confront the dualities that shape their lives.

Continue reading to uncover how Hercules' narrative sheds light on broader implications regarding human moral conflicts.

Hercules' struggle with his dual nature as both divine and mortal mirrors the human experience, shedding light on the eternal conflict between base instincts and higher ethical aspirations. This duality is not unique to Hercules alone. Still, it resonates deeply with all individuals who grapple with their inner demons while striving to embody virtues. **The tales of Hercules invite us to contemplate the complexities of our own moral conflicts**, urging us to confront our primal desires and elevate ourselves towards nobler ideals.

The clash between divinity and humanity in Hercules' narrative reflects the perpetual battle within each individual's psyche. It symbolizes the eternal tug-of-war between our innate inclinations and our aspirations for greatness. Like Hercules, we often find ourselves torn between our impulses and moral compass, navigating a path fraught with challenges and temptations. **His story is a mirror, compelling us to confront our internal struggles** and inspiring us to transcend our limitations.

By delving into the broader implications of Hercules' dual nature, we gain profound insights into the complexities of human morality. **His journey highlights the intricate dance between light and shadow within each of us**, showcasing the continuous quest for balance and harmony in a world filled with contradictions. Through

Hercules' trials, we understand that true strength lies not in physical prowess alone but in the ability to conquer our inner demons and rise above adversity.

The timeless lessons embedded in Hercules' story invite us to reflect on our moral dilemmas and ethical quandaries. They prompt us to examine our daily choices, encouraging us to align our actions with our values and beliefs. **By drawing parallels between Hercules' struggles and our own**, we can glean valuable insights into the complexities of human nature and the transformative power of virtue.

In contemplating Hercules' journey, we are reminded that **the path to greatness is often paved with obstacles** that test our resolve and character. His story serves as a beacon of hope, showing us that even in the face of insurmountable challenges, it is possible to rise above adversity and emerge victorious. **Through Hercules' example, we learn that true heroism lies not in perfection but in perseverance**, resilience, and unwavering commitment to one's principles.

As we navigate the complexities of our own moral conflicts, **Hercules' narrative offers solace and inspiration**, reminding us that even demigods are not immune to struggle. His story teaches us that true strength emanates from embracing both our divine potential and mortal frailties, finding harmony within ourselves amidst chaos. **By adopting the lessons of Hercules**, we embark on a journey of self-discovery and transformation, transcending our limitations to become the heroes of our own narratives.

Analytical Framework: Divinity and Humanity in Conflict

In dissecting Hercules' struggle with his dual nature as divine and mortal, we can employ an Analytical Framework that delves into the intricacies of this duality and its implications on human moral conflicts. This framework dissects the characteristics of divinity (immortality, supernatural powers, higher ethical standards) juxtaposed with humanity (mortality, limited physical powers, moral ambiguity), placing Hercules at the crossroads of these aspects. By examining Hercules' life through this lens, we can highlight instances where his divine and mortal natures clash or harmonize, offering insights into the broader human battle between primal instincts and the pursuit of elevated ethical objectives.

Components of the Framework:

1. Divinity Characteristics:

Divine attributes encompass immortality, supernatural abilities, and adherence to a higher ethical code. These traits exemplify ideals beyond human reach, setting a lofty standard for behavior and actions.

2. Humanity Characteristics:

Human traits involve mortality, finite physical capabilities, and ethical complexities. Humans navigate moral dilemmas within their limitations, facing inner conflicts between desires and virtues.

3. Hercules' Intersection:

Hercules embodies divine and human traits, existing at the intersection of these contrasting characteristics. His narrative illustrates the perpetual struggle between embracing his godly lineage and confronting the vulnerabilities inherent in his mortal form.

Interactions within the Framework:

The interplay between Hercules' divinity and humanity creates a dynamic tension that drives his actions and decisions throughout his legendary exploits. Moments of conflict arise when his godlike strength clashes with mortal frailty or when his noble intentions are clouded by earthly desires.

Dynamics of the Model:

This model showcases the ongoing battle within individuals to reconcile their base instincts with aspirations for ethical living. It highlights the complexity of human nature, where internal struggles mirror Hercules' conflicts between divine calling and mortal temptations.

Practical Implications:

By engaging with this framework, readers can reflect on their battles between primal urges and moral principles. Understanding how Hercules navigated his dual nature can inspire individuals to confront internal conflicts and strive for ethical growth despite imperfections.

Summary:

The Analytical Framework of Divinity and Humanity in Conflict provides a structured approach to analyzing moral dilemmas through the lens of Hercules' narrative. By exploring the interactions between divine and human characteristics in Hercules' story, readers can gain valuable insights into their struggles with base instincts versus higher ethical goals. This framework encourages introspection and contemplation on navigating the complexities of human nature while striving for personal growth and moral integrity.

Exploring Hercules' tale as a lens through which to view our own struggles between divinity and humanity enriches our understanding of the perennial moral conflicts we face. **Hercules, a figure of god and man**, embodies the perennial battle within us all: the tension between our base instincts and higher ethical aspirations. His story is not just a relic of ancient mythology but a mirror reflecting our dilemmas in striving for moral integrity.

Hercules' journey offers profound insights into man's dual nature, illustrating that our battles are not just external but internal. The myth teaches us that **the path to virtue is fraught with challenges**, and it is through overcoming these challenges that character is forged. Each of Hercules' labors is more than a feat of strength; they symbolize the trials we all undergo to reconcile our lower selves with our higher purposes.

Reflecting on Hercules' narrative encourages us to consider how we can rise above our baser instincts. It prompts a personal introspection about where we are in our journey toward ethical maturity. **Are we letting our primal desires dictate our actions, or are we striving**

towards ideals that elevate and fulfill us? Hercules' story serves as a reminder that while the struggle is universal, so too is the potential for triumph over our flaws.

Moreover, this chapter underscores the importance of understanding and empathy in navigating our moral landscapes. Just as Hercules was both divine and mortal, we, too, possess qualities that can elevate us or lead us astray. Recognizing this shared struggle fosters a deeper connection with others, encouraging a compassionate approach to personal growth and social interaction.

In weaving the rich tapestry of Hercules' exploits with the threads of modern moral inquiry, we gain insight into ancient narratives and illuminate the contours of our contemporary human condition.

This chapter invites you to reflect on your own life, to identify your labors, and to pursue them with both the strength of Hercules and the wisdom that comes from recognizing our shared human frailty.

Viewing our challenges through Hercules' dual nature gives us a more nuanced understanding of our struggles and triumphs. This perspective is enlightening and empowering, as it encourages us to face our moral conflicts with courage and resolve. Let us take inspiration from Hercules' journey, using it as a beacon to guide us in our quest for personal and ethical growth.

Chapter 8: Myths and Creative Expression

In the drowsy heat of a late afternoon in the small village of Eldora, tucked away between the whispering forests and the calm, cerulean sea, Elena found herself at the crossroads of creation and tradition. The sun hung low in the sky, casting long shadows that danced upon her canvas where myth met mortal. Her brushstrokes spoke of ancient tales, gods, and goddesses who loved and lost with a ferocity that echoed through time.

Elena's grandmother, Maria, sat nearby, weaving tales as deftly as she wove her colorful yarns into tapestries that adorned many a wall in their humble home. "The story of Artemis and Orion," Maria began with a voice smooth as the river stones, "is not just about hunt or betrayal—it's about understanding boundaries and respect." Elena listened, her paintbrush pausing mid-air as she absorbed every word.

As Maria's words flowed like a gentle brook, Elena's mind wandered to her life's parallels. Was she not also like Artemis? Guarding her art from those who wished to commercialize it and turning something pure into mere merchandise. Her heart resonated with the goddess's fierce independence and protectiveness over her domain.

Across Elena's canvas began to emerge not just images but emotions; hues of deep blue mixed with vibrant reds capturing moments of divine wrath and celestial grief. Through Artemis's eyes—portrayed with an almost haunting intensity—Elena explored her reluctance to let go and trust in what lay beyond her secluded village.

A sudden gust of wind rustled through the leaves overhead, breaking Elena's trance. She looked up to find a young boy watching curiously from a distance. He approached timidly and stood beside her easel. "Is that what anger looks like?" he asked innocently, pointing at Artemis's stormy gaze depicted on the canvas.

Elena smiled gently. "It might be," she replied thoughtfully. "But it also looks like courage." The boy nodded slowly, then ran off as if he had discovered something monumental.

As dusk approached and painted the sky pink and gold, Elena added delicate touches to Artemis's eyes—a softness that hinted at forgiveness beneath the fury. Was she not weaving her tapestry in blending myth with emotion on canvas, one that spoke not only of gods but also of a girl in Eldora who dared to dream beyond?

As night fell upon Eldora and stars began their silent vigil overhead, one might wonder how our personal myths shape our reality?

Unveiling the Creative Soul: How Myths Shape Artistic Expression

When we delve into the myths of Hercules and the Pantheon, we uncover more than just tales of heroism and divine antics; we discover a canvas for personal expression and emotional exploration. The power of these ancient narratives lies in their historical significance and their ability to inspire contemporary creativity. Through various art forms—writing, painting, or performing—individuals find unique pathways to connect with these stories, often revealing deep-seated personal interpretations and emotional responses.

The Artistic Impulse: A Gateway to Myth

Engaging creatively with mythology serves as a bridge between ancient texts and modern experiences. When someone decides to depict Hercules battling the Nemean lion through a painting or explore the complexities of Athena's wisdom in a poem, they do more than recount a story. They insert their feelings, questions, and insights into the narrative, transforming a communal myth into a personal testament. This process enriches the individual's understanding of the myth and adds a new layer of meaning to the tale itself.

Exploring Emotional Landscapes Through Myth

Personal interpretations of myths can vary dramatically from one person to another, influenced by individual experiences, cultural backgrounds, and emotional states. This diversity is what makes creative responses to mythology so profound. Each artistic creation is a window into the creator's mind, offering insights into how they view the myth and broader life themes such as heroism, justice, and morality. Engaging with these themes artistically allows individuals to explore complex emotions and life questions in a structured yet open-ended way.

Deepening Connections with Ancient Narratives

Artistic expressions do more than echo old stories; they breathe new life into them. Creators forge a deeper connection with these ancient narratives by drawing on personal experiences and emotions when engaging with mythology. This connection is not purely intellectual but intensely emotional and often spiritual. It transforms passive reading into an active dialogue between the past and present, between global mythologies and personal realities.

The Role of Community in Creative Myth-Making

While much artistic creation is a personal endeavor, community plays a crucial role in expanding and enriching this process. Sharing one's creative work can inspire others to explore their connections to mythology. Workshops, online forums, and exhibitions are just a few platforms where individuals can showcase their myth-inspired creations, sparking discussions that broaden everyone's understanding of the art and the original myths.

By encouraging creative responses to mythology through various art forms, this exploration opens up new avenues for understanding our past and ourselves. Whether through dramatic performances that revive ancient gods on modern stages or sculptures that bring mythical heroes into our physical world, each artistic endeavor adds a unique voice to the age-old tales.

As we continue this journey through myths using creative expressions as our guide, we invite you to appreciate these stories as relics of ancient civilizations and as living narratives that continue to shape our worldviews and artistic landscapes today.

In this chapter, we will delve deeper into how these processes unfold—how art becomes an exploration of self through the lens of mythology—and how you, too, might find new dimensions within yourself by engaging creatively with the stories of Hercules and his fellow gods.

Engaging in creative responses to mythology through various art forms can be a profoundly enriching and insightful experience. **Exploring mythological themes through writing, drawing, or performing allows for a personal interpretation of the stories**, fostering a deeper connection to the material. When individuals immerse themselves in creative activities inspired by myths, they can delve into their own emotions and perceptions, uncovering unique insights that may not be apparent through traditional study alone.

Writing based on mythological themes can open a world of imagination and self-expression. Whether crafting original stories inspired by ancient myths or reimagining classic tales from a modern perspective, **writing allows individuals to explore their creativity and personal connection to the myths**. Through the written word, one can delve into the nuances of character motivations, plot developments, and thematic elements, offering a fresh perspective on age-old stories.

Similarly, **drawing and visual arts** provide a unique avenue for exploring mythology. Visual representations of mythological characters, landscapes, or scenes can offer a new lens through which to interpret the stories. **Visually capturing mythological themes can deepen one's understanding of the narratives**, allowing for a more visceral and sensory engagement with the material.

Performing arts, such as acting or storytelling, offer another dimension to engage with mythology. By embodying characters from myths or narrating tales in a captivating manner, individuals can compellingly bring these ancient stories to life. **The performative aspect adds an interactive element to the exploration of mythology**, enabling participants to embody the essence of the myths they portray.

Incorporating creative responses to mythology into one's exploration of ancient tales can unlock new layers of meaning and significance. **By encouraging artistic expression inspired by myths**, individuals can tap into their creativity and emotional responses, fostering a deeper connection to the timeless stories that have captivated audiences for centuries.

Continue reading to discover how personal interpretations and emotional connections to mythological themes can be explored through creative activities.

Creative activities such as writing, drawing, or performing based on mythological themes can be powerful tools for exploring personal interpretations and emotional connections to ancient stories. Engaging in these activities allows individuals to delve deeper into the myths, uncovering unique insights and fostering a stronger bond with the material. **Expressing oneself creatively through art forms allows for a more personal and intimate exploration of mythology**, enabling individuals to connect with the stories on a profound level.

Through creative activities, individuals can reinterpret myths to resonate with their experiences and emotions. This process of reinterpretation not only enhances understanding but also reveals the timeless relevance of these ancient tales to contemporary life. **By infusing personal perspectives and emotions into artistic expressions inspired by mythology**, individuals can discover new layers of meaning within the stories, making them more relatable and impactful.

Exploring mythological themes through creative activities can be a cathartic and transformative experience. By channeling emotions and reflections into art, individuals can gain new insights into their own lives and struggles. **This process of self-discovery through creative expression allows for a deeper exploration of one's psyche and emotions,** leading to personal growth and introspection.

Creative activities based on mythology provide a safe space for emotional exploration. Individuals can confront their fears, hopes, and desires symbolically through writing, drawing, or performing. **This form of expression can help individuals process complex emotions and experiences,** offering a therapeutic outlet for self-expression and reflection.

Engaging in creative activities inspired by mythology encourages imagination and innovation. By stepping into the realm of ancient stories, individuals are free to explore limitless possibilities and unleash their creativity. **This imaginative exercise nurtures artistic skills and cultivates a sense of wonder and curiosity** about the world around us.

Through creative expression, individuals can bridge the gap between past and present, connecting with mythology's timeless themes and universal truths. Individuals can create meaningful works that resonate across time and cultures by infusing personal interpretations and emotional connections into artistic endeavors inspired by myths. **Blending ancient stories with contemporary perspectives helps keep mythology alive and relevant in our modern world.**

Incorporating creative activities into one's exploration of mythology offers a dynamic and engaging way to interact with ancient stories. **By embracing artistic expression as a tool for personal interpretation and emotional connection to myths,** individuals can unlock new depths of understanding and meaning within these timeless tales.

Artistic expression can deepen our understanding of mythology and our engagement with it. We can unlock hidden meanings, emotional connections, and individual interpretations of these ancient stories through creative activities such as writing, drawing, or performing based on mythological themes. **Engaging in artistic endeavors allows us to explore the nuances of myths beyond their surface narratives, delving into the depths of our own psyche to uncover profound insights.** By immersing ourselves in the creative process, we can forge a deeper bond with the material, allowing us to connect with the myths more intimately.

Artistic expression serves as a gateway to unraveling the layers of mythology, offering a space to breathe life into these age-old tales through our unique lens. When we write a modern-day adaptation of a myth or create artwork inspired by legendary characters, we are not merely retelling stories but infusing them with our emotions, perspectives, and experiences. **This reinterpretation brings new life into the myths, making them relevant and relatable to our contemporary lives.**

Through artistic expression, we can tap into the universal themes of mythology, uncovering truths about human nature, society, and the world at large. By exploring these themes through creative mediums, we gain a deeper understanding of ourselves and the world around us. **Artistic endeavors provide us with a mirror to reflect on our beliefs, values, and emotions,** allowing us to navigate the complexities of life through the lens of mythological narratives.

Artistic expression encourages us to embrace our creativity and imagination, inviting us to step outside the confines of reality and explore fantastical realms where anything is possible. **In this boundless space of creativity, we can unleash our innermost thoughts and feelings,** giving voice to our deepest desires and fears through art. By channeling our emotions into creative outlets inspired by mythology, we enrich our understanding of the stories and cultivate a sense of self-expression and empowerment.

Artistic exploration enables us to break free from conventional interpretations of myths. It encourages us to chart our own path through these ancient narratives. By infusing our creative works with personal anecdotes, reflections, and musings, **we breathe new life into myths that have endured for centuries,** adding complexity and richness that resonate with contemporary audiences. Through artistic expression, we can transform passive readers into active participants in the ongoing conversation surrounding mythology.

By engaging in artistic expression inspired by mythology, we open ourselves to a world of endless possibilities where imagination knows no bounds. We embark on self-discovery through writing, drawing, or performing based on mythological themes, unraveling hidden truths about ourselves and our world. In this process of creation and exploration, we deepen our understanding of mythology and forge a profound connection with the timeless tales that continue to shape our collective consciousness.

Exploring the rich tapestry of mythology through creative expression not only rejuvenates these ancient narratives but offers profound personal insights. By engaging with myths on an artistic level, individuals unlock new layers of meaning and develop a deeper, more intimate connection with these age-old stories.

Step 1: Encouraging Creative Responses to Mythology

Begin by selecting a myth that resonates deeply with you. Whether it's the trials of Hercules or the cunning of Athena, choose a theme that sparks your curiosity or emotional interest. Dive into the creative process by experimenting with various art forms—painting, writing, or sculpture. Allocate dedicated time to craft a piece that reflects your unique interpretation and emotional response to the chosen myth.

Step 2: Exploring Personal Interpretations and Emotional Connections

Once your artwork is complete, could you take a moment to reflect on it? What emotions does it stir in you? How does it connect to the mythological theme at its core? Document these reflections in a brief artist statement or reflection piece. This process deepens your understanding and prepares you to share your work with others, offering them a glimpse into your journey with mythology.

Step 3: Deepening Understanding and Personal Engagement

Engage with the creative expressions of others who have explored the same themes. Observe how their interpretations compare and contrast with yours. This step is crucial for expanding your perspective and enhancing your engagement with the myth. Participate in discussions or workshops that explore these themes through art, further enriching your experience and understanding.

Step 4: Discovering the Power of Artistic Expression

Challenge yourself to try new mediums or techniques outside your comfort zone. Reflect on how these new experiences enhance your connection to mythology and deepen your understanding of its themes. Artistic expression is not just about creating; it's about discovering and growing.

Step 5: Sharing and Inspiring Others

Consider organizing an exhibition or a creative workshop to showcase your work and that of others. Create a space for dialogue and discussion, allowing participants to explore their interpretations and emotional connections to the myths. Please encourage them to engage in their own creative processes and share their journeys, fostering a community of like-minded individuals who find common ground in the timeless stories of our ancestors.

Through this structured yet flexible approach, we pay homage to these magnificent tales and make them relevant to our modern lives. Each step builds upon the last, ensuring a comprehensive exploration of mythology through art while allowing for personal growth and community engagement. Engaging with myths in this way transforms them from distant tales of yore into living narratives that continue to inspire and shape us. By embracing creative expression as a key to unlocking the mysteries of mythology, we keep these stories alive and relevant, passing on their wisdom and beauty to future generations.

Chapter 9: Context is Key: Understanding Myths in Their Era

In the early morning light of an Athenian marketplace, the air was crisp and filled with the scent of fresh olives and salt from the nearby sea. Theron, a well-respected teacher in his mid-forties, walked among the stalls, his thoughts deep in the stories of old gods and heroes that he would later discuss in his lecture. The clatter of pottery and hushed negotiations formed a lively backdrop to his contemplations.

As he passed by a vendor selling scrolls, his eye caught a particularly ornate one depicting Zeus's thunderbolts. It reminded him of the turbulent times that shaped these ancient tales—when people sought understanding and control over nature's chaos through stories. Theron considered how these myths served not just as entertainment but as moral guides and reflections of their societal values.

Theron paused to purchase a pomegranate, breaking it open to reveal its jeweled seeds. He thought about Persephone and her annual return from Hades, which explained the seasons' cycle to an agrarian society so dependent on harvests. Each seed seemed like a story, capable of unfolding layers of meaning about life, death, and rebirth.

Later, seated on a wooden stool outside a small café sipping bitter coffee, Theron sketched notes for his upcoming class. He planned to draw parallels between the adoration of heroes in ancient myths and modern society's celebration of celebrity culture. How did Hercules' labors inspire today's tales of overcoming adversity? What could these age-old stories tell us about what we value today?

A young boy ran past, nearly colliding with Theron's table in his haste. His mother spilled apologies as she followed in quick pursuit. The momentary chaos brought Theron back from ancient Greece to present realities but also underscored how myths have always captured human experiences across time—fear, joy, and conflict.

As he watched the bustling life around him continue unabated by minor disturbances, Theron wondered: Could understanding these ancient narratives hold the key to addressing some of today's cultural conflicts? How might these old stories illuminate our path forward?

Unveiling the Tapestry of Time: Why Myths Still Matter

The tales of Hercules and his compatriots are not just stories; they are windows into the souls and societies of ancient civilizations. Understanding the context in which these myths were born and thrived is crucial to appreciating their depth and relevance.

Myths were not merely entertainment; they reflected contemporary values, fears, and aspirations. This chapter explores how the historical and cultural backdrops influenced these stories, enhancing our appreciation and connecting them to modern issues.

The ancient world was vastly different from today. Yet, it grappled with themes universal to humanity: power, justice, love, and heroism. We gain insights into why specific themes emerged by delving into the conditions that shaped these narratives. For instance, Hercules' labors can be seen as more than feats of strength—they are symbolic battles against chaos, reflecting societal struggles for order and stability.

The Power of Place and Time

Every myth is anchored in the time and place of its creation. Geographic settings, political climates, and social structures play pivotal roles in shaping the narratives. Understanding these elements allows us to see beyond the surface of the myth. It's not just about what happens in the story but why it happens and what it tells us about the people who told it.

In this chapter, we'll explore how specific historical events and cultural developments influenced the legends of Hercules and other figures from the Pantheon. For example, myths featuring strong leaders or protectors, such as Hercules, became more popular during war or upheaval. These stories offered hope and a sense of control in uncertain times.

Reflecting Ancient Values Through Modern Eyes

We can draw parallels with today's world by evaluating how myths mirrored their contemporary societies. This deepens our understanding of ancient cultures and offers fresh perspectives on current issues. Myths can act as mirrors reflecting universal concerns across ages, reminding us that while times change, human nature often remains consistent.

This exploration will also highlight how shifts in societal values can reshape myths over time. As cultures evolve, so do their stories, adapting to new morals and norms. This fluidity underscores the dynamic nature of mythology and its capacity to remain relevant across millennia.

The Ripple Effect of Contextual Awareness

Finally, fostering an appreciation for mythology's contextual roots enriches our cultural literacy, enhances our ability to engage critically with literature, and empowers us to question which aspects of our current culture might one day become myths for future generations.

In summary, by placing these age-old tales within their historical tapestries, we honor their origins and bridge the gap between past and present. This chapter sets out to show that understanding context is not just an academic exercise—it's a journey toward finding meaning in our shared human story.

Through this exploration, we aim to transform your understanding of mythology from static tales of yore to dynamic narratives that continue to shape and reflect human thought today.

Ancient myths are not merely fantastical tales; they are intricate reflections of the historical and cultural contexts in which they originated. To truly grasp the essence of these myths, one must delve into the societal norms, beliefs, and challenges of the eras in which they were born. **By understanding the environments that shaped these** narratives, we gain a deeper appreciation for their significance and relevance both then and now.

Ancient mythologies were not created in a vacuum. Still, they were influenced by their times' social, political, and religious landscapes. For example, the Greek myths were crafted in a society where gods and goddesses played integral roles in everyday life, reflecting the importance of spirituality in ancient Greece. **The stories of gods interacting with mortals may have served to explain natural phenomena or justify specific societal structures.**

Understanding these cultural nuances provides a lens through which we can interpret the morals and messages embedded in these myths.

Moreover, historical events often found their way into mythological narratives. Wars, invasions, or power shifts could be mirrored in tales of divine conflicts or heroic quests. **Myths served as a way to make sense of tumultuous times, offering hope or warnings through allegorical storytelling.**

Exploring the historical events that influenced these myths gives us insight into how ancient civilizations processed and coped with their realities.

Cultural practices also seeped into mythologies, shaping the values and virtues extolled in these stories. **The emphasis on honor in Norse mythology or the reverence for wisdom in Egyptian tales reflects the ideals held dear by those societies.** By examining how cultural norms manifest in myths, we can appreciate how these narratives reinforced societal norms and transmitted moral lessons across generations.

Unraveling the layers of historical and cultural influences behind ancient myths opens up a treasure trove of insights that enrich our understanding of these timeless

narratives. Let's explore further to uncover the hidden gems awaiting discovery.

Understanding the historical and cultural context in which myths originated is crucial for appreciating their depth and relevance. By delving into a myth's setting, we can uncover layers of meaning that might otherwise remain hidden. **Context provides the backdrop against which the characters and events of a myth unfold**, giving them a richer significance. Just as a painting gains depth from its background, so too do myths acquire new dimensions when viewed through the lens of their era.

The setting of a myth encompasses not just physical locations but also the societal norms, values, and beliefs prevalent at the time. For example, the heroic feats of ancient Greek myths were often shaped by the ideals of valor, honor, and glory that held sway in that culture. Understanding these values allows us to appreciate why specific actions were deemed heroic or villainous in those narratives. **By placing ourselves in the shoes of ancient audiences, we can better grasp the emotional impact these stories had on them.**

Cultural context also highlights why specific themes or motifs recur in myths across different civilizations. Shared experiences such as love, betrayal, power struggles, and quests for knowledge resonate universally, transcending time and place. By recognizing these common threads, we can appreciate the enduring relevance of myths in exploring fundamental aspects of the human condition. **Understanding the setting in which myths arose gives us insight into the universal truths they seek to convey.**

Moreover, situating myths within their historical context helps us grasp the political, social, and religious dynamics during their creation. Myths often served as tools for explaining natural phenomena, legitimizing rulership, or reinforcing moral codes within a society. **By recognizing these functions, we can decode these tales' underlying messages and intentions.** *The more we understand the* *world in which myths were born, the more we can extract valuable lessons and insights from them.*

Appreciating context can also lead to reevaluating our beliefs and values. By comparing ancient societal norms with contemporary ones, we may recognize continuity and change in human thought and behavior.

Examining how our perspectives differ from our ancestors can prompt us to reflect on the evolution of our moral compass and societal structures. *In this way, understanding the setting of myths becomes not just an exercise in historical inquiry but a means of self-discovery.*

In conclusion, **context is key to unlocking myths' full potential**, allowing us to appreciate their nuances and relevance across time. By immersing ourselves in the world that gave rise to these stories, we gain a deeper understanding of human nature, society, and cultural evolution. **Through contextual awareness, we bridge the gap between past and present**, enriching our interpretation of myths and drawing connections that resonate with our lives today.

Drawing parallels between ancient mythological stories and modern societal values can offer profound insights into the human experience across time. The myths of old often reflect universal themes and enduring truths that resonate with contemporary audiences. By examining how ancient civilizations grappled with concepts such as power, love, betrayal, and redemption, we can better understand our beliefs and behaviors today. **These timeless narratives serve as mirrors reflecting the complexities of human nature, providing us with valuable lessons and perspectives that remain relevant through the ages.**

Exploring the myths of Hercules and the Pantheon in their original contexts can shed light on ancient societies' core values and beliefs. These tales feature themes of heroism, sacrifice, loyalty, and destiny, mirroring the virtues prized in antiquity. **By delving into the** motivations and struggles of mythological characters, we can uncover parallels to our ethical dilemmas and personal quests for meaning. The enduring popularity of these stories attests to their ability to transcend time and speak to fundamental aspects of the human condition.

When ancient myths are compared to modern society, we may find surprising similarities in the values upheld by both eras. While the external trappings of civilization have evolved over millennia, the fundamental desires for love, power, justice, and purpose remain constant. By recognizing these shared aspirations, we can cultivate a deeper appreciation for the enduring relevance of mythology in shaping cultural identities and informing individual worldviews.

Moreover, by studying mythological stories through a contemporary lens, we can uncover layers of symbolism and allegory that speak to pressing issues. The struggles of mythical heroes against formidable foes can be metaphors for our daily battles with inner demons or external challenges. By reframing these narratives in a modern context, we can glean fresh insights into resilience, perseverance, and the quest for personal growth.

Through thoughtful reflection on ancient myths alongside current societal values, we can foster a sense of interconnectedness with our ancestors while recognizing the universality of human experiences. By bridging the gap between past and present through mythological narratives, we can glean wisdom from generations long gone and apply it to our contemporary circumstances. In this way, mythology serves as a timeless repository of human wisdom and insight that transcends cultural boundaries and speaks to humanity's shared journey through time.

Understanding the rich tapestry of historical and cultural contexts from which myths emerge deepens our appreciation and illuminates their enduring relevance. When we delve into the eras that shaped these narratives, we unlock a more profound connection with the past and, simultaneously, a more transparent reflection of our time.

Historical and cultural contexts are pivotal in grasping the true essence of mythological stories. By examining the conditions under which these myths were told, we gain insights into ancient civilizations' societal norms, challenges, and aspirations. This exploration is not merely academic but a journey that brings us closer to understanding human nature and societal evolution. As we peel back the layers of historical context, myths reveal their secrets, showing us not just the beliefs of the past but also the universal themes that transcend time.

Evaluating the setting of a myth enhances its appreciation and relevance. When we consider where and why a story was told, its characters and plots gain new dimensions of meaning. This isn't just about adding depth to our understanding—it's about connecting personally with the narratives that have shaped human thought across millennia. Such connections remind us that while our surroundings may change, human existence's fundamental questions and challenges remain constant.

Drawing parallels between ancient and modern societal values offers us a mirror of our own lives. These stories provide a framework to examine our contemporary values and ethics. What lessons do they hold for leadership, bravery, or wisdom that we can apply today? How do they address themes of love, betrayal, or ambition that are still relevant? By engaging with these ancient tales, we are prompted to reflect on our own society and personal lives in an introspective and enlightening way.

This chapter has aimed not just to inform but to inspire—a call to view ancient myths not as relics of the past but as living narratives that continue to shape and reflect our world. As we move forward, let's carry with us the understanding that myths are more than stories; they are a powerful lens through which we can view the past and the present, understand more deeply who we are, and perhaps guide who we wish to become.

In embracing these timeless tales, we not only preserve them but also allow them to evolve, finding new meanings and lessons relevant to our time and perhaps to future generations. Let this journey through mythology invigorate your curiosity and broaden your perspectives, enriching your understanding of the ancient world and our place today.

Chapter 10: The Joy of Myth: Making Learning Lively

In the dim, cluttered study, where the scent of old books mingled with the faint aroma of cedarwood, Eleanor sat at her heavy oak desk. She was surrounded by piles of texts and scrolls, each page whispering tales from ancient mythologies that echoed through time. As a high school mythology teacher, she found herself at a crossroads, seeking ways to breathe life into these age-old stories for her students, who seemed more captivated by their phones than by the exploits of gods and heroes.

Outside, the wind rustled through the autumn leaves, a reminder of Persephone's descent into Hades and the ensuing barrenness that swept over the earth. This natural cycle of life and death mirrored Eleanor's struggle to keep mythology relevant in the minds of young learners. The challenge was to teach and ignite a flame of curiosity that would burn steadily and brightly.

As she sifted through an ancient Greek text, her fingers brushed over the delicate pages, each touch bringing forth images of ancient civilizations that valued storytelling as a vessel for wisdom and morality. She pondered integrating interactive technology into her lessons—perhaps virtual reality scenarios where students could experience Odysseus' journey first-hand or podcasts where they could listen to dramatized versions of myths as modern-day radio plays.

Her cat, Apollo—named after the god of prophecy—leapt onto her desk, breaking her train of thought. He purred softly as he nestled amongst the scattered papers. Moments like this reminded Eleanor why she loved teaching mythology; it connected her to something timeless and universal.

Yet she knew she needed a new approach to help her students see these connections themselves.

The clock struck three in the afternoon—a dull chime marking time's slow march—and Eleanor rose from her chair to stretch. The room felt smaller somehow as if it were closing in on her with all its weighty expectations. She gazed out the window at students walking across campus beneath fiery red maples, their laughter piercing through their otherwise mundane routine.

Would these children ever grasp how myths shaped civilizations? How do they weave together not just tales but also cultures? Could they learn joyfully without sacrificing depth? These questions haunted Eleanor as she returned to her desk, determined yet uncertain. How could one ensure these stories are preserved in translation between generations?

Unleashing the Power of Myth in Modern Learning

The joy and intrigue that mythology can inject into education must be explored. As we delve into the world of Hercules and the vast Pantheon, the potential to transform dry historical narratives into vibrant tales of heroism and human folly becomes evident. This chapter aims to bridge the gap between mere factual learning and a more dynamic, engaging educational experience that sparks a lasting passion for ancient stories.

Why Learn Myths?

At its core, mythological study offers more than an understanding of ancient cultures; it provides insight into the human condition, societal values, and personal identity. By infusing educational practices with lively methodologies, we can elevate myths from ancient relics to living lessons that resonate with contemporary audiences. The challenge, however, lies in how these stories are taught.

Engaging Methods: A Sneak Peek

Exploring dynamic methods of teaching mythology is not merely about making learning fun but ensuring it is profoundly impactful.

Techniques such as storytelling sessions, interactive role-plays, and integration of digital media are not just tools but gateways to deeper comprehension and appreciation. These approaches allow learners to immerse themselves in the complexities of mythic narratives, seeing past the ancient language to the timeless dilemmas they present.

Sustaining Curiosity

The initial fascination with mythic tales like those of Hercules or Zeus is natural; sustaining that interest is where true educational artistry comes in. This chapter will explore how continuous engagement tactics can be developed within educational frameworks to keep students curious about mythology.

Balancing Fun and Facts

The critical balance between enjoyment and education ensures that learners retain the factual integrity of myths while reveling in their enchanting narratives. We will discuss strategies to maintain this balance, helping educators design informative and enjoyable lessons.

The Broader Picture

Reflecting on previous chapters, it's clear that understanding Hercules or any other mythological figure requires immersion into their world—understanding their challenges, victories, and transformations. The methods discussed here aim to educate and inspire a connection with these characters, enabling readers to draw parallels between ancient myths and modern life.

Lifelong Engagement with Myths

Ultimately, by making mythological education enjoyable and informative, we aim to foster a lifelong engagement with these stories. This enduring interest ensures that the wisdom of the ancients continues to enlighten future generations, keeping alive the lessons learned from Hercules' strength or Athena's wisdom through engaging narratives.

In essence, this chapter does not just advocate for a revival of interest in mythology; it provides a roadmap for transforming mythological education into a captivating journey that respects its roots while thriving in contemporary culture. Through this approach, learners can appreciate the stories and their relevance and impact on today's world.

Learning and teaching about mythology can be a vibrant and engaging experience, far removed from traditional education's dull and dry methods.

Educators and learners alike can unlock a world of wonder and wisdom by infusing creativity and dynamism into the exploration of myths. One approach is to incorporate interactive activities such as role-playing, where students embody mythological characters, bringing the stories to life in a tangible way. **This hands-on approach deepens understanding and fosters a sense of connection with the ancient tales.**

Visual aids can also play a crucial role in making mythology more accessible and captivating. From illustrations to multimedia presentations, these tools can help learners visualize the fantastical worlds of gods and heroes, making the stories more relatable and engaging. **By appealing to different learning styles**, educators can ensure that all students can connect with the material in a way that resonates with them.

Storytelling is another powerful tool for bringing mythology to life. Whether through dramatic readings or interactive storytelling sessions, sharing myths orally can evoke emotions and create lasting impressions. **Storytellers** can spark curiosity and ignite a passion for further exploration by immersing listeners in the narrative.

Incorporating creative **projects** into mythological studies can also enhance learning experiences. From crafting visual representations of myths to writing modern adaptations of ancient stories, these projects encourage critical thinking and imaginative expression. **By engaging in hands-on activities**, students deepen their understanding of mythology and develop essential skills such as creativity and problem-solving.

Interactive discussions provide a platform for students to share their perspectives, ask questions, and engage in meaningful dialogue about myths. These conversations enrich the learning experience and foster a sense of community and collaboration among learners. **By creating a space for open exchange**, educators empower students to think critically and explore the nuances of mythological narratives.

Embracing dynamic and enjoyable methods for learning mythology invites us to delve deeper into these timeless tales, fostering a lifelong love for the wisdom they hold within.

Fostering sustained curiosity and enthusiasm in mythological studies is essential for a deep and lasting connection to these timeless tales. By approaching mythology with a sense of wonder and excitement, we can unlock the profound wisdom embedded within these stories. **Encouraging a continuous exploration of myths** helps us uncover layers of meaning and relevance that resonate with our lives today.

Engaging with myths as living narratives rather than historical accounts allows us to find personal connections and draw parallels to our experiences. By delving into the character's motivations, the challenges they face, and the lessons they learn, we can extract valuable insights that enrich our understanding of human nature and the world around us. **Approaching mythology with a curious mind** opens up a treasure trove of knowledge waiting to be discovered.

Creating an environment that nurtures curiosity is critical to sustaining interest in mythological studies. Whether through interactive storytelling sessions, group discussions, or creative projects inspired by myths, there are countless ways to keep the flame of curiosity burning. **Encouraging questions and fostering a sense of wonder** cultivates a deep-rooted passion for learning that transcends traditional boundaries.

Embracing myths' multifaceted nature allows us to explore different perspectives and interpretations, keeping our curiosity alive and thriving. Each retelling, discussion, and reflection on a myth brings new insights and revelations that fuel our enthusiasm for continued exploration.

Approaching myths with an open mind enables us to see beyond the surface level and uncover hidden gems of wisdom.

Maintaining enthusiasm for mythological studies requires dedication and commitment, but the rewards are boundless. The joy of unraveling complex narratives, deciphering symbolic meanings, and connecting with characters from ancient times can be immensely fulfilling.

Embracing mythology as a lifelong journey ensures we always have new discoveries and lessons.

By staying curious, open-minded, and enthusiastic about myths, we enrich our lives and contribute to keeping these ancient stories alive for future generations. The joy of myth lies not only in the tales themselves but in the continuous process of exploration and interpretation that they inspire. Let's embrace this wondrous journey with open hearts and eager minds, ready to uncover the magic within each myth we encounter.

We aim to cultivate a lifelong engagement with myths by creating an educational environment that balances enjoyment with informative content. By integrating **interactive activities** into the learning process, we can transform the study of mythology from a passive exercise into an exciting adventure. Incorporating **role-playing games**, where students embody mythological characters and navigate through challenges, can bring these ancient tales to life in a way that resonates deeply with learners.

Visual aids such as artwork, maps, and multimedia presentations can enhance the educational experience by providing **visual context** to the discussed stories. By appealing to different learning styles, we ensure all students can engage meaningfully with the material. Encouraging **group discussions and debates** allows for a dynamic exchange of ideas, fostering critical thinking and deepening understanding.

Infusing the learning environment with a sense of **wonder and curiosity** is crucial to maintaining enthusiasm for mythological studies. We create an atmosphere that sparks intellectual growth and creativity by posing thought-provoking questions and encouraging students to explore different perspectives. **Encouraging research projects** where students delve deeper into specific myths or cultural contexts broadens their knowledge. It instills a sense of ownership over their learning journey.

In this vibrant educational setting, balancing fun and academic rigor is essential. While we want to make learning about myths enjoyable, we must also ensure that students gain **substantial knowledge** about the subject matter. By structuring lessons that combine **entertainment with education**, we can guarantee that students are not only having fun but also acquiring valuable insights into the world of mythology.

By creating an educational environment that values both enjoyment and informative content, we set the stage for a lifelong exploration of myths. Through engaging activities, visual aids, stimulating discussions, and a blend of entertainment and education, we can instill a lasting passion for these timeless stories in our students. This approach ensures that the wisdom contained within myths continues to resonate with learners long after they have left the classroom, fostering a deep appreciation for the cultural significance of these ancient tales.

Throughout this exploration of mythology, we have embraced methods that make learning about ancient legends informative and profoundly enjoyable. By integrating dynamic teaching approaches, we've seen how mythology can captivate and inspire, fostering a sustained curiosity that transforms occasional interest into a lifelong journey of discovery.

The Power of Engaging Education

The techniques discussed here underscore the importance of balancing enjoyment with educational rigor. This balance must tip fairly in one direction; instead, it should harmoniously blend the joy of the stories with the depths of their historical and cultural significance. This approach ensures that learners of all ages remain engaged and eager to delve deeper into the mythical narratives that have shaped civilizations.

Lifelong Engagement with Mythology

Our focus on creating an inviting educational environment serves a dual purpose: it makes learning more appealing and memorable. The stories of Hercules, gods, and demigods are not just tales of the past but lessons in human values, struggles, and triumphs. By presenting these stories in a manner that resonates with today's audiences, we bridge the gap between ancient and modern worlds, making the wisdom of the old relevant to contemporary life.

Connecting Past with Present

The strategies discussed here aim to revitalize the rich tapestry of mythology in ways that respect its complexity while making it accessible to everyone. Through interactive storytelling, multimedia resources, or thought-provoking discussions, we bring these ancient characters to life, allowing them to teach us about resilience, heroism, and the enduring human spirit.

This book has journeyed through the intricate lives and adventures of mythological figures, highlighting their legendary exploits and impact on our current understanding of culture and history. By engaging with these stories, readers gain knowledge and an enriched perspective on life itself.

Let us carry forward this blend of education and enjoyment, ensuring that the timeless tales of mythology continue to inspire and educate future generations. Through this journey, may you find both knowledge and joy in history's vast, echoing halls.

Epilogue

Embracing the Timeless: Carrying Ancient Wisdom into Tomorrow

As we draw the curtain on our journey through the legends of Hercules and his pantheon companions, I hope that these stories have not merely entertained but also enriched your understanding of how ancient narratives can illuminate our present and guide our future. The myths we've explored are far from being just relics of the past; they are vibrant, living scripts that continue to shape our worldviews and ethical landscapes.

The real-world applications of these tales are manifold. By delving into Hercules's struggles and triumphs, we gain insights into human resilience and the importance of courage in the face of adversity—qualities that are as essential today as they were in antiquity. These stories encourage us to look within and confront our trials with similar courage, reminding us that every challenge we face is an opportunity for growth.

Throughout this book, we've seen how Hercules' adventures reflect broader human concerns—justice, power, betrayal, and redemption—deeply resonating with contemporary life. These narratives encourage us to question and redefine what it means to be a hero in our own lives.

To **apply these ancient insights**, consider how you might embody Hercules' perseverance in your pursuits. Whether tackling professional challenges, personal projects, or advocating for justice, let his determination inspire you to push through obstacles with integrity and strength. Furthermore, educators and storytellers can use these myths to foster discussions about morality, leadership, and the complexities of human nature in classrooms or creative works.

While I have endeavored to present these stories with depth and accessibility, I acknowledge that no book can cover every nuance. Future explorations could dive deeper into lesser-known myths or examine the archaeological contexts that have shaped our understanding of these tales. The canvas of mythology is vast and varied, inviting endless discovery.

Please take these stories into your heart and let them stir you into action or contemplation. Let them be a mirror in which you see not just the feats of demigods but also the reflection of your potential for greatness.

Let's carry forward the torch of insight lit by Hercules' enduring legacy to illuminate our paths and warm those who walk beside us in this ever-unfolding tale of human endeavor.

"Mythology is not just a collection of stories told but a reflection of our collective truths narrated through time." - Unknown.

By embracing these age-old narratives, we weave ourselves into the rich tapestry of human history and ensure that its lessons do not fade into obscurity but continue to guide us in wisdom and virtue.

References

Dasgupta, R. (2023). Patron's Desk'. Globsyn Management Journal, 17(1/2), III.

Understanding the Car Horn Emoji: A Guide. https://bosshorn.com/blogs/blog/car-horn-emoji

Guardians of the Galaxy Tree: Unveiling the Iconic Marvel Symbol - galaxystore.vn. https://galaxystore.vn/guardians-of-galaxy-tree/

Angel Number 1010 | Embracing Transformation and Fulfillment. https://thefifthelementlife.com/angel-number-1010/

The Casino Family: Generational Gambling Traditions – Virtual Egion. https://virtualegion.com/the-casino-family-generational-gambling-traditions/

Tutorials Unveiled: Master the Information Forum – Newlyn. https://newlyn.info/tutorials/

The True Measure of Courage: The Ability to Face and Overcome Fear. https://www.themotivationmasterclass.com/post/the-true-measure-of-courage-the-ability-to-face-and-overcome-fear

When Walking Away Works – Mens Toolbox. https://menstoolbox.org/when-walking-away-works-2/

Why Is It So Hard To Find Your Purpose In Life? The Eye-Opening Truth - lifefoodice. https://lifefoodice.com/why-is-it-so-hard-to-find-your-purpose-in-life-the-eye-opening-truth/

Dreaming of a Snake Biting You: Discover the Spiritual Meaning and Interpretation - A-Z Animals. https://a-z-animals.com/articles/dreaming-of-a-snake-biting-you-discover-the-spiritual-meaning-and-interpretation/

Book Moreh Derekh: The Rabbi's Manual of the Rabbinical Assembly (English, Hebrew and Hebrew Edition) → Download and Print PDF, Abstract, Specs, Data Sheet, Read Online and more. https://www.booksnbibles.com/moreh-derekh-the-rabbi-manual-the-rabbinical-assembly-english-hebrew-and-hebrew-edition/

Dreamwork: Unlocking the Messages of Your Subconscious Mind – Pretty Spirits. https://prettyspirits.com/blogs/blog/dreamwork-unlocking-the-messages-of-your-subconscious-mind

Caesar Baronius. https://www.nboratory.org/pages/saints/www.oratoriosanfilippo.org/baronio.html

Yellow Hematite Quartz Moons - Embrace the power of the sun | GemStals. https://www.gemstals.com/product-page/yellow-hematite-quartz

Production | www.renard-music.com. http://www.renard-music.com/production

Decoding Work-Related Stress: The Power Of Cognitive Behavioural Hypnotherapy" - CBH. https://bohangar.com/uncovering-the-causes-of-stress-and-anxiety-at-work-a-comprehensive-analysis/

Explainer Videos For Software Tools | Explainer Video Company. https://thevideoanimationcompany.com/explainer-videos-for-software-tools/

How GenUnity Empowered Changemakers in Pursuit of Housing Justice. https://www.genunity.org/case-studies/how-genunity-empowered-changemakers-in-pursuit-of-housing-justice

WinStars - FileRax. https://filerax.com/winstars

Unveiling the Power of Characterisation in Literature: A Comprehensive Exploration - Story Arcadia. https://storyarcadia.com/unveiling-the-power-of-characterisation-in-literature-a-comprehensive-exploration/

Digital Learning Magazine | Asia's First Monthly Magazine on Education. https://digitallearning.eletsonline.com/about-us/

Literary Landmarks: Visiting the Inspirational Settings of Famous Novels. https://highwaydreams.net/literary-landmarks-visiting-the-inspirational-settings-of-famous-novels/

The Fascinating History of Commemorative Coins - All My Treasures. https://allmytreasures.com/the-fascinating-history-of-commemorative-coins/

Exploring the Enigma of Artistic Experience: A Comprehensive Guide – Cultural Exploration. https://www.laguiahotelera.com/exploring-the-enigma-of-artistic-experience-a-comprehensive-guide/

The Epic Face-off: Megan vs Mittens - Unleashing the Power Struggle of 2023 - Board Playing. https://boardplaying.com/megan-vs-mittens-power-struggle-of-2023/

Solar Power and Indigenous Knowledge Systems: Traditional Wisdom in Modern Applications - Solar Panels Inverters & Installation | PowerSmart Solutions. https://www.powersmartsolutions.com.au/solar-power-and-indigenous-knowledge-systems-traditional-wisdom-in-modern-applications/

Meditations by Marcus Aurelius - Thinkers Books. https://thinkersbooks.com/index.php/2023/12/16/meditations-by-marcus-aurelius/

The D. H. Chen Foundation Scholarship. https://www.dhcfscholarship.com/scholars/winnie-cheng/

You Are Your Own Greatest Teacher Quotes - Words On Images. https://wordsonimages.com/image/You-Are-Your-Own-Greatest-Teacher-Quotes.SqwSm

Book Holy Bible - Containing Both the Old and the New Testaments - Red Letter Edition (King James Version) New Clarified Reference Bible → Download and Print PDF, Abstract, Specs, Data Sheet, Read Online and more.

https://www.booksnbibles.com/holy-bible-containing-both-the-old-and-the-new-testaments-red-letter-edition-king-james-version-new-clarified-reference-bible/

Unveiling the Mysteries Behind ovestæ: Everything You Need to Know - Vamonde. https://www.vamonde.com/ovestae-2/

Aroma Thyme Bistro | Hudson Valley Restaurant | Blogs - AROMA THYME, HUDSON VALLEY FARM TO TABLE RESTAURANT. https://www.aromathymebistro.com/blogs/a-day-of-discovery-in-apulia-unveiling-the-culinary-and-enological-treasures

Abbey Road Art | Landscape. https://abbeyroadart.com/abbey-road-art/tag/landscape

Reading Twin Passions. http://readingonlinenovel.com/Twin_Passions/p

Download Sodium MOD 1.21, 1.20.6 → 1.16. https://bobbacraft.com/sodium/

An Appraisal of the Bilingual Language Production System: Quantitatively or Qualitatively Different from Monolinguals | Ian FitzPatrick. http://ianfitzpatrick.eu/publication/handbook/

Wonderful Meaning Of Christmas Tree In The Bible. https://www.prayerslife.com/meaning-of-christmas-tree-in-the-bible/

Exploring the Surprising Benefits of Reading Romance Novels. https://romancereader.com/the-emotional-and-psychological-benefits-of-romance-novels/

Biblical Meaning of 87: Unlocking its Spiritual Significance. https://biblewithus.com/biblical-meaning-of-87/

Humane Society Of The Treasure Coast. https://bonevoyagedogrescue.com/humane-society-of-the-treasure-coast/

World Contraception Day 2023. https://www.biomedcentral.com/p/world-contraception-day-2023?fbclid=IwAR2kUbzYMdNMxgSbKagrBVdV3-vxa5Cba7AC0gZa-nixnYFY6jbLBDte8Q8#:~:text=World%20Contraception%20Day%20(WCD)%20takes[1]

1.   https://www.biomedcentral.com/p/world-contraception-day-2023?fbclid=IwAR2kUbzYMdNMxgSbKagrBVdV3-vxa5Cba7AC0gZa-nixnYFY6jbLBDte8Q8#_853ae90f0351324bd73ea615e6487517__4c761f170e016836ff84498202b99827__853ae90f0351324bd73ea615e6487517_text_43ec3e5dee6e706af7766fffea512721_World_0bcef9c45bd8a48eda1b26eb0c61c869_20Contraception_0bcef9c45bd8a48eda1b26eb0c61c869_20Day_0bcef9c45bd8a48eda1b26eb0c61c869_20_84c40473414caf2ed4a7b1283e48bbf4_WCD_9371d7a2e3ae86a00aab4771e39d255d__0bcef9c45bd8a48eda1b26eb0c61c869_20takes_c0cb5f0fcf239ab3d9c1fcd31fff1efc_their_0bcef9c45bd8a48eda1b26eb0c61c869_20sexual_0bcef9c45bd8a48eda1b26eb0c61c869_20and_0bcef9c45bd8a48eda1b26eb0c61c869_20reproductive_0bcef9c45bd8a48eda1b26eb0c61c869_20health

Can you Undo Dreadlocks? - Mets Minor League Blog. https://metsminorleagueblog.com/can-you-undo-dreadlocks/

Humanity in Action Fellowship | Pace Prestigious Awards and Fellowships. https://awardsandfellowships.pace.edu/project/humanity-in-action-fellowship-2/

O. Althobaiti, M. A. (2023). The Evolution of European Fairy Tales: A Comparative Analysis of the Grimm Brothers and Hans Christian Andersen. https://core.ac.uk/download/578588757.pdf

Exploring the Time of Amos: Map of Ancient Judah's Landscape | Kids Maps. https://www.kidsmaps.com/judah-at-the-time-of-amos

Kennedy, B. A. (2005). ... of butterflies, bodies and biograms ... Affective Spaces in Performativities in the Performance of Madama Butterfly. Edinburgh University Press EBooks. https://doi.org/10.3366/edinburgh/9780748635030.003.0010

Teaching Students With Learning Disabilities: A Step-By-Step Guide For Educators – Academy educations. https://academyeducations.com/2023/12/03/teaching-students-with-learning-disabilities-a-step-by-step-guide-for-educators.html

About Us. https://www.kutyslifestyle.online/p/about-us.html

Omolara, I. (2023). The Method of Teaching English Using Music. https://core.ac.uk/download/553346290.pdf

The Great Irish History Book – Creative Irish Gifts. https://www.creativeirishgifts.com/products/lg511

The Impact of Interactive Workshops in Learning - livingworkshop.net. https://livingworkshop.net/the-impact-of-interactive-workshops-in-learning/

Jernsletten, K. (. (2012). The hidden children of Eve : Sámi poetics guovtti ilmmi gaskkas. https://core.ac.uk/download/392163916.pdf

Don't miss out!

Visit the website below and you can sign up to receive emails whenever Myrddin Sage publishes a new book. There's no charge and no obligation.

https://books2read.com/r/B-A-JBAOB-RFGQD

Connecting independent readers to independent writers.

Also by Myrddin Sage

Mythic Japan: Unlocking the Legends of Gods and Heroes
Echoes of Enchantment: Navigating the Magic of Celtic Mythology
Echoes of Valhalla: Unveiling the Modern Wisdom of Norse Myths
Gods Among Us: The Power and Intrigue of Roman Mythology
The Sword and the Sage: Unveiling the Truth of Excalibur and Merlin
Myth Unleashed: Rediscovering the Legends of Hercules and the
Pantheon

About the Author

At 67, Myrddin Sage steps into the spotlight as a newly published author, bringing a tapestry of rich life experiences and a vibrant imagination. His journey from a Navy Veteran to a Retired Dispatcher of Messengers has endowed him with profound insights into human cultures and the natural world. As Myrddin introduces his debut novel, he shares a narrative infused with wisdom, whimsy, and a deep respect for the interconnectedness of life. Drawing on his academic background and extensive travels, Myrddin's work explores themes of adventure, discovery, and the transformative power of knowledge. With his first publication, he proves that new chapters can be embarked upon at any stage of life, inspiring readers with the message that it is always the right time to follow one's passions.